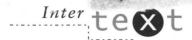

The Language of Poetry

This accessible satellite textbook in the Routledge INTERTEXT series is unique in offering students hands-on practical experience of textual analysis focused on poetry. Written in a clear, user-friendly style by an experienced writer and practising teacher, it links practical activities with examples of texts. These are followed by commentaries and suggestions for research. It can be used individually or in conjunction with the series core textbook, *Working with Texts: A core book for language analysis*.

Aimed at A-Level and beginning undergraduate students, *The Language of Poetry*:

- focuses on the 'look, the sound, the movement and the appeal of poetry
- uses clusters of poems to highlight differences in structure, tone, quality and form
- explores historical, contemporary, regional and social differences in language and style
- combines a highly individual and fascinating selection of poems from the canonical to the fringe, among them an Old English lament, a haiku and a poem by Benjamin Zephaniah
- includes a selection of suggestions for project work
- has a comprehensive glossary of terms

John McRae is Special Professor of Language in Literature Studies at the University of Nottingham. He has been at the forefront of work on the language and literature interface for many years and is the co-author of *The Routledge History of Literature in English*.

Inter te**X**t

The Intertext series

◎ **Why does the phrase 'spinning a yarn' refer both to using language and making cloth?**

◎ **What might a piece of literary writing have in common with an advert or a note from the milkman?**

◎ **What aspects of language are important to understand when analysing texts?**

The Routledge INTERTEXT series will develop readers' understanding of how texts work. It does this by showing some of the designs and patterns in the language from which they are made, by placing texts within the contexts in which they occur, and by exploring relationships between them.

The series consists of a foundation text, *Working with Texts: A core book for language analysis*, which looks at language aspects essential for the analysis of texts, and a range of satellite texts. These apply aspects of language to a particular topic area in more detail. They complement the core text and can also be used alone, providing the user has the foundation skills furnished by the core text.

Benefits of using this series:

◎ **Unique** – written by a team of respected teachers and practitioners whose ideas and activities have also been trialled independently

◎ **Multi-disciplinary** – provides a foundation for the analysis of texts, supporting students who want to achieve a detailed focus on language

◎ **Accessible** – no previous knowledge of language analysis is assumed, just an interest in language use

◎ **Comprehensive** – wide coverage of different genres: literary texts, notes, memos, signs, advertisements, leaflets, speeches, conversation

◎ **Student-friendly** – contains suggestions for further reading; activities relating to texts studied; commentaries after activities; key terms highlighted and an index of terms

The series editors:

Ronald Carter is Professor of Modern English Language in the Department of English Studies at the University of Nottingham and is the editor of the Routledge INTERFACE series in Language and Literary Studies. He is also co-author of *The Routledge History of Literature in English*. From 1989 to 1992 he was seconded as National Director for the Language in the National Curriculum (LINC) project, directing a £21.4 million in-service teacher education programme.

Angela Goddard is Senior Lecturer in Language at the Centre for Human Communication, Manchester Metropolitan University, and was Chief Moderator for the project element of English Language A-Level for the Northern Examination and Assessment Board (NEAB) from 1983 to 1995. Her publications include *The Language Awareness Project: Language and Gender*, vols I and II, 1988, and *Researching Language*, 1993 (Framework Press).

First series title:

Working with Texts: A core book for language analysis
Ronald Carter, Angela Goddard, Danuta Reah, Keith Sanger, Maggie Bowring

Satellite titles:

The Language of Sport
Adrian Beard

The Language of Newspapers
Danuta Reah

The Language of Advertising: Written texts
Angela Goddard

The Language of Humour
Alison Ross

The Language of Poetry
John McRae

The Language of Fiction
Keith Sanger

Related titles:

INTERFACE series:

Variety in Written English
Tony Bex

Literary Studies in Action
Alan Durant and Nigel Fabb

Language, Literature and Critical Practice
David Birch

English in Speech and Writing
Rebecca Hughes

A Linguistic History of English Poetry
Richard Bradford

Feminist Stylistics
Sara Mills

The Language of Jokes
Delia Chiaro

Language in Popular Fiction
Walter Nash

The Discourse of Advertising
Guy Cook

Textual Intervention
Rob Pope

The Language of Poetry

- John McRae

LONDON AND NEW YORK

First published 1998
by Routledge
11 New Fetter Lane, London EC4P 4EE

Simultaneously published in the USA and
Canada
by Routledge
29 West 35th Street, New York, NY 10001

Reprinted 1999

*Routledge is an imprint of the Taylor & Francis
Group*

© 1998 John McRae

Typeset in Stone Sans/Stone Serif by
Solidus (Bristol) Limited

Printed and bound in Great Britain by TJ
International Ltd, Padstow, Cornwall

*British Library Cataloguing in Publication
Data*

A catalogue record for this book is
available from the British Library

*Library of Congress Cataloguing in Publication
Data*

McRae, John.
    The language of Poetry/John McRae.
        p.   cm. – (Intertext)

    Includes index.

    1. English language – Style.
2. English poetry – History and criticism.
3. English language – Versification.
4. Discourse analysis, Literary.
5. Style, Literary. 6. Poetics.
I. Title. II. Series: Intertext (London,
England)
    PE1421.M39   1998
    808. 1 – dc21
                                        97-17316

ISBN 0–415–16928–3

I shall invent a new game; I shall write bits of slang and poetry on slips and give them to you to separate.

George Eliot, *Middlemarch*

contents

acknowledgements

Maya Angelou, 'Women Work', from: *And Still I Rise*. By kind permission of Virago Press.

Anon., 'Deor's Lament', from *An Anthology of Old English Literature* by Charles W. Kennedy. Copyright © 1960 by Charles W. Kennedy. Reprinted by kind permission of Oxford University Press, Inc.

Simon Armitage, 'Let This Matchstick Be a Brief Biography' in *The Dead Sea Poems*. By kind permission of Faber & Faber.

W.H. Auden, 'Stop All the Clocks', from *Collected Poems* by W.H. Auden, edited by Edward Mendelson. Copyright © 1940 and renewed 1968 by W.H. Auden. Reprinted by permission of Random House Inc.

Louise Bennett, 'Colonization in Reverse', originally published in *Selected Poems*, edited by Mervyn Morris, Kingston, Jamaica.

Edward Clerihew Bentley, 'Clive' originally published in *Biography for Beginners* (1905). Publisher unknown.

Valerie Bloom, 'Yuh Hear Bout', from *Grandchildren of Albion*, edited by Michael Horovitz, New Directions. By courtesy of Valerie Bloom. Originally published in *Touch Mi, Tell Mi* by Bogle l'Ouverture, 1983/90.

Robert Crawford, 'Nec Tamen Consumebatur', from *A Scottish Assembly*, Chatto & Windus, 1990.

e.e. cummings, 'ygUDuh' and 'The Moon's A Balloon', from *Selected Poems 1923–58*.

Emily Dickinson, 'Much Madness . . .'; 'Because I could not stop for Death . . .'; 'I Sing to use the Waiting . . .'; 'A narrow Fellow in the Grass . . .'. Reprinted by kind permission of the publishers and the trustees of Amherst College from *The Poems of Emily Dickenson*, edited by Thomas H. Johnson, Cambridge, Mass.: The Belknap Press of Harvard University Press. Copyright © 1951, 1955, 1979, 1983 by the President and Fellows of Harvard College.

T.S. Eliot, *The Hollow Men* (last two lines). Reprinted by courtesy of Faber & Faber and Harcourt Brace Jovanovich Inc.

Gavin Ewart 'Office Friendships' from *Selected Poems 1933–93*, Hutchinson Books Ltd, Chatto & Windus. By kind permission of Margo Ewart.

Nissim Ezekiel, 'Goodbye Party for Miss Pushpa T.S.' from *Collected Poems 1952–88*. Originally published in *Hymns in Darkness*, Oxford University Press, India, 1976.

Robert Frost, *Stopping by Woods on a Snowy Evening*, from *The Poetry of*

Robert Frost, edited by Edward Connery Latham © 1951 by Robert Frost. © 1923 © 1969 by Henry Holt & Co. Inc. Reprinted by permission of Henry Holt & Co. Inc.

Lorna Goodison, *I Am Becoming My Mother*, New Beacon Books.

Alfred Perceval Graves, *Father O'Flynn*, reprinted by kind permission of J.M. Dent.

Tony Harrison, 'Them and [uz]', from *More Poems*, published by Jonathan Cape and Holt Rinehart & Winston. Reprinted by kind permission of Gordon Dickerson for Tony Harrison.

Seamus Heaney, 'Digging' from *Poems 1965–1975*. © 1980 by Seamus Heaney. Reprinted by permission of Faber & Faber and Farrar, Straus & Giroux Inc.

A.E. Housman, 'Because I Liked You Better' from *More Poems*. Reprinted by permission of The Society of Authors as the literary representative of the Estate of A.E. Housman.

Langston Hughes, 'I Too Sing America' from *Selected Poems* by Langston Hughes. Copyright 1926 Alfred A. Knopf Inc. and renewed 1954 by Langston Hughes. Reprinted by permission of the publisher.

Rebecca Hughes, 'Divergence', reprinted by kind permission of the author.

Rudyard Kipling, *If*. By courtesy of A.P. Watt Ltd. on behalf of The National Trust.

Philip Larkin, 'This Be the Verse', from *High Windows*, reprinted by kind permission of Faber & Faber.

Tom Leonard, *Jist Ti Let Yi Know*, reprinted by permission of the author. First appeared in the sequence *Bunnit Husslin*, Third Eye Centre, Glasgow 1975. Reprinted in *Intimate Voices: Writing 1965–83* Galloping Dog Press, Newcastle 1984. Reprinted by Vintage Press 1995.

Amy Lowell (d. 1943), *Patterns*.

John McRae, 'Haiku', published in the British Haiku Society anthology, *Fire*, 1993. Reprinted by kind permission of the author and the British Haiku Society. 'Elijah and Isaac', published in *Not Love Alone*, GMP, London, 1985. Reprinted by kind permission of the author and GMP Publishers Ltd.

Roger McGough, '40-Love', from *Penguin Modern Poets 10*, 1971. Reprinted by permission of A.D. Peters & Co. Ltd.

Muhammad Haji Salleh, 'A Star-Petalled Flower Falls', from *Time and Its People*, reprinted by permission of the author.

Stevie Smith, 'Not Waving But Drowning', from *Collected Poems of Stevie Smith*. Copyright (c) 1972 by Stevie Smith. Reprinted by kind permission of New Directions Publishing Corp.

Stephen Spender, *I Think Continually of Those Who Were Truly Great*, single line reprinted by courtesy of Faber & Faber.

Dylan Thomas, 'Do Not Go Gentle Into That Good Night' from *The Poems of Dylan Thomas*. Copyright 1952 by Dylan Thomas. Reprinted by permission of J.M. Dent and New Directions Publishing Corps.

Malachi Edwin Vethamani, 'It Was A Wondrous Sight' published in *South-East Asia Writes Back*, Skoob Pacifica Anthology No. 1, Skoob Books, 1993. Reprinted by kind permission of the author and Skoob Books Publishing Ltd.

William Carlos Williams, 'This is Just To Say', from *Collected Poems 1909–1939, vol. 1*. Copyright 1938 by New Directions Publishing Corp. Reprinted by permission of Carcanet Press and New Directions Publishing Corp.

W.B. Yeats, 'The Second Coming'. Reprinted with permission of Simon & Schuster from *The Collected Works of W.B. Yeats*, vol. 1.: *The Poem*; revised and edited by Richard J. Finneran. Copyright 1924 by Macmillan Publishing Company; copyright renewed (c) 1952 by Bertha Georgie Yeats; and by permission of A.P. Watt Ltd on behalf of Michael Yeats.

Benjamin Zephaniah, 'As a African', originally published in *Inna Liverpool* by the African Arts Collective, Liverpool 1988/90. Reprinted by kind permission of Benjamin Zephaniah, copyright (c) 1992.

Routledge has made every effort to trace copyright holders and to obtain permission to publish extracts. Any omissions brought to our attention will be remedied in future editions.

The look

First of all, what is poetry?

◎ words with a frame round them
◎ 'what oft was thought, but ne'er so well express'd'
   (Alexander Pope, *An Essay on Criticism*, 1711)
◎ 'the *best* words in the best order'
   (Samuel Taylor Coleridge, from *Table Talk* magazine, 1827)
◎ the words of the current number-one hit
◎ boring old-fashioned soppy stuff
◎ the words inside birthday cards.

Which of these signifies *poetry* to you? Tick one or two – add more if you want to.

In this unit we are going to look at a range of texts, and try to decide what makes them poetry, and see how we react to them subjectively and objectively. To allow the focus to be on the texts themselves, titles and authors are listed at the end of each unit, with a complete list of all the poems quoted appearing at the end of the book (p. 143).

So what makes poetry good or bad?

Activity

Look at these lines and grade them on a 1 to 10 scale, where you think 1 is bad, 6 quite good, 10 really good.

Text: Poems (i)–(x)

(i)   The trumpets sounded,
Saint Peter said, 'Come.'
The pearly gates opened
And in walked Mum.

(ii)   'Tis said that some have died for love

(iii)   I've measured it from side to side:
'Tis three feet long, and two feet wide.

(iv)   What I like about Clive
Is that he is no longer alive.
There is a great deal to be said
For being dead.

(v)   God save our gracious Queen,
Long live our noble Queen,
God save the Queen.

(vi)   There was an old man of Thermopylae,
Who never did anything properly;
But they said, 'If you choose
To boil eggs in your shoes,
You shall never remain in Thermopylae.'

(vii)   Fear no more the heat o' th' sun
Nor the furious winter's rages;
Thou thy worldly task hast done,
Home art gone, and ta'en thy wages.

(viii)   Then hurrah! for the mighty monster whale,
Which has got seventeen feet four inches from tip to tip of a tail!
Which can be seen for a sixpence or a shilling,
That is to say, if the people all are willing.

(ix)   How do I love thee? Let me count the ways.
I love thee to the depth and breadth and height
My soul can reach, when feeling out of sight
For the ends of Being and ideal Grace. [. . .]
I love thee with a love I seemed to lose
With my lost saints - I love thee with the breath,
Smiles, tears, of all my life! - and, if God choose,
I shall but love thee better after death.

(x)   They come as a boon and a blessing to men,
The Pickwick, the Owl, and the Waverley pen.

Did any of them make 10 out of 10? Give reasons for your choices. (Discuss the results in groups, if possible.)

List some of the *negative* aspects in the texts and some more *positive* ones.

Negative   Positive

....

....

....

Commentary

First we might react to the subject matter − so many of them seem to be about death. But they range from fairly banal (i) to serious (vii, ix). Probably (vii), (ii) and (ix) would be the highest-rated for most readers. Compared with the others, they have a range of reference (past, present, future) and touch on more than one idea. In short, they give the reader the chance to explore the potential meanings and resonances in the text, rather than just one level of simplistic meaning or effect.

The length of the lines might add something to the appeal of (ii) and (viii) in particular − compare the short lines of (i). The final line of (i) creates an effect of **bathos**, and might even make the reader laugh: (iv) and (vi) do this more deliberately. Text (v) does none of these, and perhaps sounds least 'poetic'. **Rhyme** can reinforce the effect created by the sound of the text − we will see more of this. But what of 'poetic' language? Look at (ii): instead of saying 'some people have died for love' it is distanced by the words ''Tis said', and another level is introduced − the words, the order of the words, the sound, all come into the equation. Text (vii) is similarly a bit removed from everyday language, with 'thou', 'art', 'o' th'', etc., which sound 'poetic' − they are older forms of language. Look also at contrasts: hot/cold, life/death, past/present, which give the poem its movement.

Activity

In Text: Poems (xi)−(xvii) are some lines which have been considered 'great', poetry? How do they compare with the ones you have just read?

3

Text: Poems (xi)–(xvii)

(xi) Who ever loved, that loved not at first sight?

(xii) Sweet Thames! run softly, till I end my song.

(xiii) Shall I compare thee to a summer's day?
Thou art more lovely and more temperate.

(xiv) Tyger! tyger! burning bright
In the forests of the night,
What immortal hand or eye
Could frame thy fearful symmetry?

(xv) Summer is i-cumen in,
Lude sing, cuccu!
Groweth seed and bloweth med
And springth the wode nu.

(xvi) When lilacs last in the dooryard bloomed,
And the great star early drooped in the western sky at night,
I mourned, and yet shall mourn with ever-returning spring.

(xvii) The woods decay, the woods decay and fall,
The vapours weep their burthen to the ground,
Man comes and tills the field and lies beneath,
And after many a summer dies the swan.

Commentary

Try reading some of these aloud: *sound* makes a contribution to *sense*. Which lines do you find the most musical?

There is a wider range of sounds, emotions and rhymes in these samples: happiness, sadness, power, regret, awe, and more. Repetition features in several of them, reinforcing the effects. The texts make us read them in different ways, by the form, the language they use, the sounds, and even the references (the Thames, the tiger). We construct our readings out of all these influences, plus what we bring to the text. Part of us takes the text subjectively, reacting emotionally, and part can be objective, thinking about the specific devices, tricks and techniques the poet uses.

For example: unanswered rhetorical questions (xi, xiii, xiv), exclamations (xii, xiv, xv), and images (the first line of (xvi) really means 'last spring', but makes an image of it, combining time, home, and a sense of loss) – all these contribute to how the texts work.

If we try grading these lines on the same scale as before is it easier, or not, to separate them into 'good' or 'bad'? Some of them will simply appeal to you subjectively more than others – just enjoy them!

Extension

Try the same sort of thing with any song lyrics you know well. What makes some work more for you than others?

Keep some of these ideas in mind: we will look back at some of these questions as we go on.

Activity

We are going to move on to what a text looks like, and how that affects its 'poetry'.

Where do you think you might find this?

> This is just to say I have eaten the
> plums that were in the icebox and
> which you were probably saving for breakfast
> Forgive me they were delicious
> so sweet and so cold

◎   How can you tell if it's spoken or written?
◎   What is the essence of the message? Could it be said in fewer words? What words would you have used?
◎   So, what are the other words there for? (Padding, politeness, covering something up, . . . etc.)
◎   Realistically, who might be writing, and to whom?
◎   Is it a poem? Why/why not?

Try writing it *as* a poem.

Commentary

How is it now different from the version above? There can be an infinite number of variations experimenting with different possibilities: change the words or keep them the same; emphasise the forgiveness, or the taste, rather than the information; do it in the shape of a plum; use rhyme and put it into stanzas; give it a title.

Activity

Now you can check out the 'real' poem (Text: Poem (xviii)). Look at how it works, compared to your version, and to the 'note' version above. What similarities and differences are there?

Text: Poem (xviii)

(**xviii**)   *This Is Just to Say*

I have eaten
the plums
that were in
the icebox

and which
you were probably
saving
for breakfast

Forgive me
they were delicious
so sweet
and so cold

Commentary

It is often the very look of the text that conditions our response to it. At first this text looked like a note on the fridge door or left on the kitchen table. But the words say a lot more than just 'sorry I ate the plums'. And would you have said 'Forgive me' – it seems a bit strong.

It is very often worthwhile thinking about what we ourselves would have written and comparing it with what the author wrote; that can give us an insight into what the text is doing. The word 'icebox', for instance, is more common in American English than British, and yes, the author is American.

The simple fact of rearranging the words in any way shows something of how texts work differently in different shapes or with a different word order. Putting it into three stanzas influences such things as line length, the emphasis given to some words, like 'saving'.

Who might be speaking/writing to whom is often an interesting question to wonder about, although often it cannot be answered.

The word 'so' in the last two lines is a *subjective* intensifier: it makes us taste the plums more directly than, for example, 'very sweet and very cold'.

Activity

We can try another exercise in rewriting now. Look at Text: Poem (xix). What makes it 'work' for you?

Text: Poem (xix)

(xix)	40	–	LOVE
	middle		aged
	couple		playing
	ten		nis
	when		the
	game		ends
	and		they
	go		home
	the		net
	will		still
	be		be
	tween		them

◎ Try writing this as sentences. What is lost, and what gained, if anything?

◎ What do you think it is about most: tennis, space, love, age ... or what?

How modern do you think these two texts are? Tick a date for each:

	19th century	1920s	1930s	1940s	1950s	1960s	1970s	1980s	1990s
'This is Just to Say'	....	....	....	....	....	....	....	....	....
'40–Love'	....	....	....	....	....	....	....	....	....

'This is Just to Say' was published in 1923, '40–Love' in 1971. Probably 'This Is Just to Say' feels more modern than that.

Activity

Rewriting is one of the main techniques we can use when working with poetic texts. Sometimes it will simply 'frame' or 'de-frame' the text; often it will help us unravel complicated **syntax**, as in this moment when Eve bites the apple in the Garden of Eden (Text: Poem (xx)).

Text: Poem (xx)

(xx)   'What hinders, then,
To reach, and feed at once both body and mind?'
So saying, her rash hand in evil hour
Forth-reaching to the fruit, she plucked, she eat;
Earth felt the wound, and Nature from her seat,
Sighing through all her works, gave signs of woe
That all was lost.
[. . .] all heaven
Resounded, and had earth been then, all earth
Had to her centre shook.

Try putting some lines into more 'usual' English; then read the two versions aloud. For example, the last three lines might read 'all heaven felt the shock,/And if earth had existed then,/It would have been shaken to its core.

What words do you find that are clearly old forms? Are there any rhymes which would not work in modern English?

John Milton's *Paradise Lost*, from which that extract is taken, is an **epic** poem, with rich, sonorous, ten-syllable lines in clearly defined **rhythm**.

Count the number of **syllables** in each line; just sound the syllables as you read. Very often you will find ten-syllable lines throughout your reading of poetry; **iambic pentameter**, i.e. 5×2 syllables, is considered the closest to English rhythms of speech. Iambic is short/long ($\cup$ —), one syllable lightly stressed, the other with a heavier emphasis, and the line sounds short/long five times to make iambic pentameter. It is always worth checking the syllable count — shorter or longer lines may create different effects.

Extension

We can conclude this look at shape and form with two contrasting short texts (Text: Poems (xxi)–(xxii)).

What does the shape or the look of the text give to these? How would they be different in another form (single lines, or dialogue, for instance)?

Text: Poems (xxi)–(xxii)

(**xxi**)   the fire that burned
               in a loving hearth
    turned to ashes in the morning
	(**xxii**) If I should meet thee
	    After long years,
	    How should I greet thee?
	    With silence and tears.

The first is a **haiku**, a Japanese form based on the use of seventeen syllables, often 5/7/5, but here 4/5/8, expressing the 'zen' or essence of a passing moment. The second is a stanza with a very regular **rhyme scheme**: a b a b.

Questions that might come into our minds as we read these two texts could cover things like: is there word play on heart/hearth; would another organisation of the lines make a difference; who answers the question; what had happened between 'I' and 'thee'?

These questions are not necessarily to be answered. They can be *explored*, thought about, discussed. We, as readers, can decide for ourselves what a text makes us wonder or what it makes us think about.

What we have been considering in this unit covers the *look* as well as the content of texts. With any text we read, we have to make some decisions:

- what it looks like (a recipe, a horoscope, an advertisement, a poem, etc.)
- what the form tells us
- what the language tells us
- what more we need to know (or want to know).

These questions could be asked about *all* the texts we have already looked at. For example:

- Which one looks as if it was on a gravestone?
- Which one might be from an advertisement?
- Which ones look old and which modern? How can you tell?
- Are there any you recognise?
- Which do you take as serious, and which not?

You could now seek out some other samples of what might broadly qualify as poetry. Try greetings cards, pop songs, women's magazines, newspapers, advertisements as sources. *But* also look out one or two 'real' poems: ask parents or friends if they can remember poems or poetic lines. Collect them for future reference, and see where you would place them on the 1–10 scale.

How much of your reaction to these texts is *subjective*, how much *objective*, do you think? And how much does a poem need to be serious?

With the next two similar-looking examples (Text: Poems (xxiii)–(xxiv)), how can you tell whether they are serious or not?

Text: Poems (xxiii)–(xxiv)

(xxiii)	'Twas brillig and the slithy toves Did gyre and gimble in the wabe: All mimsy were the borogoves, And the mome raths outgrabe.	**(xxiv)**	Ben Battle was a soldier bold And used to war's alarms: But a cannon-ball took off his legs, So he laid down his arms.

Do you need to know the strange words in the first one? Does it work grammatically – subject before verb, verb before object, for instance? Would rewriting it with 'real' words make it better?

In the second one, what makes it memorable for you – the rhyme, the **pun**, the **alliteration**, or nothing at all?

We have already come across rhyme, rhythm, alliteration, **stanzas**, **free verse**, epic, and even a haiku. Check these back in the texts you have read so far.

Sources

(i) Anonymous obituary verse; (ii) William Wordsworth, extract from ' 'Tis Said That Some Have Died for Love' (1800); (iii) William Wordsworth, extract from 'The Thorn' (early draft, 1798); (iv) Edward Clerihew Bentley, 'Clive' from *Biography for Beginners* (1905); (v) Extract from UK national anthem (18th century); (vi) Edward Lear, extract from *One Hundred Nonsense Pictures and Rhymes* (1872); (vii) William Shakespeare, extract from *Cymbeline* (1610); (viii) William McGonagall, extract from 'The Famous Tay Whale' (1883/4); (ix) Elizabeth Barrett Browning, extract from *Sonnets from the Portuguese*, 43 (1850); (x) Anonymous advertising slogan (1880s); (xi) Christopher Marlowe, extract from *Hero and Leander* (*publ.* 1598); (xii) Edmund Spenser, extract from *Prothalamion* (1596); (xiii) William Shakespeare, extract from *Sonnets*, 18 (*c.* 1594); (xiv) William Blake, extract from 'The Tyger' from *Songs of Innocence and Experience* (1794); (xv) 13th-century English lyric; (xvi) Walt Whitman, extract from 'When Lilacs Last in the Dooryard Bloomed' (1865); (xvii) Alfred, Lord Tennyson, extract from 'Tithonus' (1833); (xviii) William Carlos Williams, 'This Is Just to Say' (1923); (xix) Roger McGough, *40 – Love* (1971); (xx) John Milton, extract from *Paradise Lost* (1667); (xxi) John McRae, 'The Fire That Burned' (1993); (xxii) George Gordon, Lord Byron, extract from 'When We Two Parted' (*c.* 1820); (xxiii) Lewis Carroll, extract from *Through the Looking Glass* (1871); (xxiv) Thomas Hood, extract from 'Faithless Nelly Gray' (1820s).

The sound

From the look of the text, we move on to the sound - not just 'music' or rhyme, but also the voices in a text.

We have already seen, in 'This Is Just to Say', that the question can often be asked, who is speaking, to whom? In 'How Do I Love Thee?' (p. 2) the answer would probably be a lover to the one he or she loves, for instance.

What can you tell about the *voice* of the poem, or the *I* or *you/thee* of the poem in Text: Poems (i)–(xii)?

Text: Poems (i)–(xii)

(i)   O what can ail thee, knight-at-arms,
Alone and palely loitering?

        (ii)   Farewell! thou art too dear for my possessing,
And like enough thou know'st thy estimate.

(iii)   Yestre'en the Queen had four Marys,
The night she'll hae but three;
There was Mary Seaton, and Mary Beaton,
And Mary Carmichael, and me.

        (iv)   I am the enemy you killed, my friend.

(v)   Your lips, on my own, when they printed 'Farewell',
Had never been soiled by the 'beverage of hell';
But they come to me now with the bacchanal sign,
And the lips that touch liquor must never touch mine.

        (vi)   I come from haunts of coot and hern,
I make a sudden sally
And sparkle out among the fern,
To bicker down a valley. [. . .]
For men may come and men may go,
But I go on for ever.

(vii)   I have been half in love with easeful Death

        (viii)   Had we but world enough, and time,
This coyness, lady, were no crime.

(ix)   I bring fresh showers for the thirsting flowers,
From the seas and the streams.

        (x)   With how sad steps, O Moon, thou climb'st the skies!
How silently, and with how wan a face!

(xi)   What heart could have thought you? –
Past our devisal
(O filigree petal!)

        (xii)   They are all gone into the world of light,
And I alone sit lingering here.

Each of these has an **addresser**, the voice or the 'I' of the text, and most also have an **addressee**, to whom the words are spoken.

Examine what the language tells you in each, and see if you can identify the following addressers:

a Queen's maid   a brook or stream   the wind   a dead soldier

and the following addressees:

an alcoholic   a snowflake   the moon   a soldier   a lost love   a shy lover.

What do you make of the others? Who do you think are 'all gone', for instance, in the last extract?

Commentary

Very often, these questions do have a (fairly) clear answer but not always, as we saw in 'This Is Just to Say'. It is not easy to say precisely who is asking the 'knight-at-arms' what can ail him. But it is important to check out what we *can* tell, and move on from there: to the knight's answers, for instance (in Unit 6, p. 83–4).

The addressers and addressees can be anyone or anything, real or imagined: so what is the function of this kind of address? When, as we saw, the writer addresses the 'Sweet Thames' he might be suggesting the river's eternal flow . . .

In (xii), for example, 'they' are all the poet's friends and acquaintances. The lines open up ideas of solitude, loneliness, loss, but a different kind of solitude from (i), which leaves the question hanging, unanswered. Text (vii) gives an idea of languor, with a positive/negative **paradox** making Death seem positive; (iv) gives a context of war, but with the paradox of enemy/friend. Paradoxes and contrasts, often in **binaries**, often give a line a sense of being a dialogue, as we shall see.

Activity

Each text will lead us into different areas. In Text: Poem (xiii), what can you tell about the speaker and who/what he is addressing?

Text: Poem (xiii)

> (xiii)   Little Fly,
>   Thy summer's play
>   My thoughtless hand
>   Has brush'd away.
>
> 5   Am not I
>   A fly like thee?
>   Or art not thou
>   A man like me?
>
>   For I dance,
> 10 And drink, & sing,
>   Till some blind hand
>   Shall brush my wing.
>
>   If thought is life
>   And strength & breath,
> 15 And the want
>   Of thought is death;
>
>   Then am I
>   A happy fly,
>   If I live
> 20 Or if I die.

Commentary

The 'I' has clearly killed the fly, and this leads to the series of questions, not all of which are answered directly. The tenses of the verbs are significant, moving from present perfect in the first stanza to present, and on to future, before returning to the present tense.

Little linking words make a difference here: 'Till' (line 11) moves the ideas on; 'If' (line 13) questions; 'Then' (line 17) leads to the conclusion. But it all depends on 'If' (lines 13, 19, 20).

Binaries are often a vital tool in seeing how a text works. They are pairings, like I/thee, and can be opposites, complementary, convergent or divergent. Common examples are male/female, day/night, black/white.

The use of binaries as a starting point for examining the themes and contrasts in any text gives us a clear basis for any discussion, without the risk of becoming too abstract or abstruse. As well as man/fly, what other possible binaries can you find in this poem?

We could ask whether, overall, the poem is happy or sad, whether life or death predominates, and where it leaves us between binaries. The text leaves us between life and death, between 'thought' and 'want of thought', so that we as readers have to think about the issues and questions raised, evaluating that 'If'.

Look at the 'If' again in Text: Poem (xiv):

Text: Poem (xiv)

> (xiv)   If I should die, think only this of me:
> That there's some corner of a foreign field
> That is for ever England.

Although there are only three lines, we can tell quite a lot about the 'I' — probably male, a soldier, English, and resigned to possible death overseas in battle. But he doesn't actually die, even though dying is the key idea. We can ask all sorts of questions about 'I' and find the answers implied between the lines; to ask who he is speaking to might not give such a clear answer. And if we wonder when he wrote, we might judge that there is a kind of patriotic feeling here, brought out in the binary 'foreign field'/'England', that is a bit old-fashioned. (The poem is from the period of the First World War.)

Look back at some of the texts so far, and decide again how modern, or not, you think they might be. What clues do you find in the language?

Activity

We have seen how little words like 'till' and 'if' can be important. We are going to look at some more 'little' words.

In the two verses in Text: Poem (xv), what do you think the missing words might be?

17

Text: Poem (xv)

> (xv)   Day after day, day after day,
> We stuck, _____ breath _____ motion;
> As idle as a painted ship
> Upon a painted ocean.
>
> Water, water, everywhere
> And all the boards did shrink;
> Water, water, everywhere
> _____ any drop to drink.

Commentary

Most people would say 'And not a drop to drink', but, in fact, it is 'Nor any drop to drink', and 'nor breath nor motion'. Frequently we take such little words for granted, but the poet's choice of words could surprise us. Look out for unexpected word choice: thinking what *you* might have written will often help to emphasise the unexpectedness of the words you read.

We have already noticed the use of rhyme: sometimes the rhymes are obvious, sometimes less so. The rhymes here are simple: 'motion'/ 'ocean' and 'shrink'/'drink'. The rhythm too is simple: the verses can be scanned in short and long syllables. Read the stanzas aloud to hear the short/long contrasts:

```
— ∪ ∪ — — ∪ ∪ —            — ∪ — ∪ — ∪ —
∪ — ∪ — ∪ — ∪              ∪ — ∪ — ∪ —
∪ — ∪ — ∪ — ∪ —            — ∪ — ∪ — ∪ —
∪ — ∪ — ∪ — ∪              ∪ — ∪ — ∪ —
```

These stresses give us a way to read the poem, but we would not always want to be strictly tied to rhythm when we read. Some texts flow more, perhaps, as in Text: Poem (xvi), because the lines are longer, and the rhyme carries the sound and the sense.

Text: Poem (xvi)

(xvi)   Let not ambition mock their useful toil,
Their homely joys, and destiny obscure;
Nor grandeur hear with a disdainful smile,
The short and simple annals of the poor.

The boast of heraldry, the pomp of pow'r,
And all that beauty, all that wealth e'er gave,
Awaits alike th' inevitable hour,
The paths of glory lead but to the grave.

Notice that the rhyme need not be exact – 'obscure'/'poor'.

Would you say these two stanzas were better read fast or slow? What words and sounds influence the way you would read them?

There is a balance between little or **'function'** words, often to be read as 'short' and consequently not noticed, and **'content'** words, like 'ambition' and 'destiny' (in the first two lines).

Take a minute or two to look at some questions about the linguistic links in these two stanzas.

◎   'Their' (lines 1 and 2) refers forward, to what in line 4? What is the subject of 'mock' (line 1)? And the object? Is 'obscure' (line 2) a noun, a verb, or an adjective?

◎   What is the subject of 'Awaits' (line 7)? (There is more than one, despite the singular form of the verb!)

◎   If you were to add a **connector** before 'The paths of glory' (line 8), what might it be – 'as', 'because', 'since', 'perhaps', 'if'?

These are the kinds of operation you have to perform with poetry texts: they help you to go beyond the initial impact or effect, which may be purely subjective, and see how the text actually *works* in terms of syntax, voice, vocabulary, and so on.

Doing these linguistic operations brings you closer into the text, and lets you decide what these two stanzas are about for you – ambition, the poor, life and death, or what?

19

Describing a text

You can sometimes judge something about the tone of a text fairly quickly. Is it light or serious, matter-of-fact, seductive, nostalgic, questioning, or some other adjective? Look back and see which texts you can judge in this way.

Of course, the tone might depend on performance, on how the words are said. It will often be useful to try saying them in different ways, to see how the tone affects the way the text works.

Some rhymes can be deliberately funny – we saw 'Thermopylae'/ 'properly' earlier. Gilbert and Sullivan's comic operas use rhyme for comic effect, as in Text: Poem (xvii):

Text: Poem (xvii)

> (**xvii**)   I'm very well acquainted too with matters mathematical,
> I understand equations, both the simple and quadratical,
> About binomial theorem I'm teeming with a lot o' news -
> With many cheerful facts about the square of the hypotenuse.

A whole poem can play lightly with ordinary words (and ordinary experience), using that kind of witty rhyme. Check out the rhymes in Text: Poem (xviii):

Text: Poem (xviii)

> (**xviii**)   Eve is madly in love with Hugh
> And Hugh is keen on Jim.
> Charles is in love with very few
> And few are in love with him.
>
> 5   Myra sits typing notes of love
> With romantic pianist's fingers,

Dick turns his eyes to the heavens above
Where Fran's divine perfume lingers.

Nicky is rolling eyes and tits
10 And flaunting her wiggly walk.
Everybody is thrilled to bits
By Clive's suggestive talk.

Sex suppressed will go berserk.
But it keeps us all alive.
15 It's a wonderful change from wives and work
And it ends at half past five.

Commentary

If you ask some questions about where this is set, and the tone, you might decide that the point of view is masculine (maybe even objectionably so!), the tone light (but what about the unexpected mention of 'wives' – line 15?). But then, words like 'us all' (line 14) involve the reader in what's happening, and we might wonder how much we are being brought into a sexist attitude that we don't necessarily share. We can identify the situation and the characters, but the poet makes us think about how much we would want to identify ourselves with it.

Activity

Now compare the serious rhythm and less flippant rhymes in Text: Poems (xix)–(xx).

Text: Poems (xix)–(xx)

(**xix**)   Two loves I have, of comfort and despair
         Which like two spirits do suggest me still;
         The better angel is a man right fair,
         The worser spirit a woman colour'd ill;
5   To win me soon to hell, my female evil
         Tempteth my better angel from my side,
         And would corrupt my saint to be a devil,
         Wooing his purity with her foul pride.
         And whether that my angel be turn'd fiend,
10   Suspect I may, yet not directly tell;
         But being both from me, both to each friend,
         I guess one angel in another's hell.
         Yet this shall I ne'er know, but live in doubt,
         Till my bad angel fire my good one out.

(**xx**)   What passing-bells for these who die as cattle?
         – Only the monstrous anger of the guns.
         Only the stuttering rifles' rapid rattle
         Can patter out their hasty orisons.
5   No mockeries now for them; no prayers nor bells,
         Nor any voice of mourning save the choirs, –
         The shrill, demented choirs of wailing shells;
         And bugles calling for them from sad shires.
         What candles may be held to speed them all?
10   Not in the hands of boys, but in their eyes
         Shall shine the holy glimmers of good-byes.
         The pallor of girls' brows shall be their pall;
         Their flowers the tenderness of patient minds,
         And each slow dusk a drawing-down of blinds.

◎   The traditional way of marking rhyme schemes, for these two poems, would be:

      'Two loves . . .'   a b a b c d c d e f e f g g
      'What passing-bells . . .'   a b a b c d c d e f f e g g

Are any of the rhymes slightly odd, like 'obscure'/'poor' which we saw earlier?

◎   Pick out some of the binaries in the first poem: man/woman, ...

◎   'But' (line 11) and 'Yet' (line 13) change the direction of the text, introducing a contrast, and then moving back from it.

◎   What is happening in lines 5–10 opens the problem up a bit more: the female love is trying to entice the male one away. And it looks as if she succeeds: the 'I' is still uncertain.

◎   Do the last two lines resolve the situation, or does the final rhyming **couplet** leave that 'doubt' in the reader's mind?

Commentary

1   You can tell in 'Two loves . . .' from the very beginning what the poem is about. The 'I' has two loves, one seen positively, one more negatively. The second poem is more complex. The answer to the question in line 1 is, for example, not an answer, but a substitute for the 'passing bells' there should have been.

What then contrasts with the bells? There are a great many sounds, all violent sounds of war.

The war is balanced with references to religion and funerals: the title of the poem is 'Anthem for Doomed Youth' – how appropriate do you find it?

2   The last six lines stress *light*, where the first eight stressed *sound*. Can you find other binaries?

Each part is set in a different place: the first part in the battlefields of France, the second back in the 'sad shires' of England. The last line suggests many things – grief, respect, the ongoing sense of loss in the future.

3   Do you find the tone of the two poems similar or different? Pick out words, phrases, or lines which give you the particular tone of each one.

4   Each of these poems has fourteen lines, and is, therefore, a **sonnet**. We will read quite a few. There is a structure to the sonnet, often of eight lines (**octet**), then six (**sestet**), but there are many variations on this.

These two sonnets set up a situation in the first eight lines (the two loves; the contrast between war and a religious service). The first tells the imagined story of 'I''s two loves together, then moves back and forth between the two of them and 'I', until, after line 8, the idea of 'fiend' comes in; but, of course, 'I' does not know, and the last six lines emphasise doubt, with 'Till' (line 14) leading to some hope for the future. 'Anthem for Doomed Youth' is more clearly octet and sestet; the first reflecting sounds, the sestet light and darkness. It is more regular in its structure – sadness and futility emerging as the keynotes, rather than the doubt and ambivalence of 'Two loves . . .'

Extension

You might like to look out for more examples of the things we have been looking at in this unit: texts where the sound and the sense go closely together (TV adverts are a good example), texts where little words make a big difference. Or contrasting the tone of two seemingly similar texts, such as the war poems 'If I should die . . .' and 'Anthem for Doomed Youth'.

On another level, do you know any other sonnets? Check them out to see if they are at all similar to the two you have just read.

And you might like to check out the kind of things you find written on war memorials and compare them with 'Anthem for Doomed Youth'.

All of these things can contribute a strong beginning to a Poetry Journal of your own, in which you can relate things in this book to other texts you find, or your reflections on them. You might even put in a poem or two of your own.

Sources

(i) John Keats, extract from 'La Belle Dame sans Merci' (1819/20); (ii) William Shakespeare, extract from *Sonnets*, 87 (*c.* 1594); (iii) Anonymous, 'The Queen's Marys' (16th century); (iv) Wilfred Owen, extract from 'Strange Meeting' (*c.* 1917); (v) George W. Young, extract from 'The Lips that Touched Liquor Must Never Touch Mine' (*c.* 1900); (vi) Alfred, Lord Tennyson, extract from 'The Brook' (1864); (vii) John Keats, extract from 'Ode to a Nightingale' (1819); (viii) Andrew Marvell, extract from 'To His Coy Mistress' (1670s); (ix) Percy Bysshe Shelley, extract from 'The Cloud' (1820); (x) Philip Sidney, extract from *Astrophel and Stella*, 31 (*publ.* 1591); (xi) Francis Thompson, extract from 'To a Snowflake' (1890s); (xii) Henry Vaughan, extract from 'They Are All Gone' (1655); (xiii) William Blake, 'The Fly' from *Songs of Innocence and Experience* (1789/94); (xiv) Rupert Brooke, extract from 'The Soldier' (1915); (xv) Samuel Taylor Coleridge, extract from 'The Rime of the Ancient Mariner' (1798); (xvi) Thomas Gray, extract from 'Elegy Written in a Country Churchyard' (1750/1); (xvii) W.S. Gilbert, extract from *The Pirates of Penzance* (1879); (xviii) Gavin Ewart, 'Office Friendships' (1966); (xix) William Shakespeare, *Sonnets*, 144 (*c.* 1594); (xx) Wilfred Owen, 'Anthem for Doomed Youth' (1918)

three

The movement

We have seen that often the words of a text move it backwards and forwards in time and space. Looking back, you will notice there are a lot of repetitions, often in the form of **parallelism**, in many poetic texts. That is a fairly simple device. The syntax, as we have seen, can become pretty complex. This can happen over a couple of lines, or through a whole poem.

Text: Poem (i) uses *time-words* to create its structure. As you read, pick out any references to time that you can find.

Text: Poem (i)

> (i)   When I have fears that I may cease to be
>   Before my pen has gleaned my teeming brain,
>   Before high-pilèd books, in charact'ry,
>   Hold like rich garners the full-ripened grain;
> 5   When I behold, upon the night's starred face,
>   Huge cloudy symbols of a high romance,
>   And think that I may never live to trace
>   Their shadows, with the magic hand of chance;
>   And when I feel, fair creature of an hour!
> 10   That I shall never look upon thee more,
>   Never have relish in the faery power
>   Of unreflecting love; then on the shore
>   Of the wide world I stand alone, and think
>   Till love and fame to nothingness do sink.

◎   Trace through words like *when* and *then*: how do they affect the whole poem?

◎   What precisely is 'I' afraid of? Is it simply death? 'May' and 'before' might influence this.

◎   What words in lines 2 and 4 have a suggestion of harvesting? How do they relate to the overall ideas of the poem?

◎   What binaries do you find?

◎   Who (or what) might 'thee' ('fair creature of an hour' – line 9) be, in your opinion? It could be a real person (his beloved, for example), or something more abstract like inspiration.

Commentary

1   The 'When . . . When . . . when . . . then' structure (lines 1, 5, 9, 12) takes us from 'fears that I may cease to be / Before . . .' to the sense of solitude and nothingness at the end. It is not death itself that 'I' fears, but that he *may* die *before* writing the books he has in his 'teeming brain' (line 2).

2   The earthly harvesting level seen in lines 2 and 4 ('gleaned', 'garners', 'grain' – all similar-sounding words) contrasts with the

starry romantic level – the 'fair creature' could be his beloved, any beauty, or anything treasured. Again there is a contrast between now and the unknown future ('never', 'Never' – lines 10–11). So the poem moves between binaries of present and future, the real and the still unachieved, presence and absence, everything and nothing, life and death, creativity ('harvesting') and emptiness.

3   Lines 2–3 mean producing books ('in charact'ry' means in writing); 'books hold my matured thoughts' is the sense.

4   Are 'love' and 'fame' actually equated with 'nothingness'? They are related in the overall balance between life and death, present and future, actual and possible; 'I' wants both love and fame, but knows how difficult it is to reach either.

5   Some words and phrases could be interpreted in many ways – 'high romance', 'magic hand', for instance. Do you prefer to see them as realistic, or as images?

6   Take the first line,

> When I have fears that I may cease to be,

and the last line,

> Till love and fame to nothingness do sink.

Compare and contrast them. How much do they reflect the whole poem?

7   The first line represents the fears; the last line the possible consequence of his early death – that he will achieve nothing.

Keats died when he was 24; so he might have been right to have these fears, although he certainly did achieve fame. We will take this idea up again later.

Activity

In Text: Poem (ii) just compare the first line and the last line, before you read the whole text.

27

Text: Poem (ii)

> (ii)   Not, I'll not, carrion comfort, Despair, not feast on thee;
>   Not untwist – slack they may be – these last strands of man
>   In me or, most weary, cry *I can no more*. I can;
>   Can something, hope, wish day come, not choose to be.
> 5   But ah, but O thou terrible, why wouldst thou rude on me
>   Thy wring-world right foot rock? lay a lionlimb against me? scan
>   With darksome devouring eyes my bruisèd bones? and fan,
>   O in turns of tempest, me heaped there; me frantic to avoid thee and flee?
>   Why? That my chaff might fly; my grain lie, sheer and clear.
> 10 Nay in all that toil, that coil, since (seems) I kissed the rod,
>   Hand rather, my heart lo! lapped strength, stole joy, would laugh, cheer.
>   Cheer whom, though? the hero whose heaven-handling flung me, foot trod
>   Me? or me that fought him? O which one? is it each one? That night, that year
>   Of now done darkness I wretch lay wrestling with (my God!) My God.

Commentary

We will go through this in detail with questions to look at and comments to consider.

Lines 1–4

- ◎ Read only the first two lines to begin with. One word is repeated four times. In the next two lines a contrasting word is repeated three times. Use these two words to balance what 'I' is saying he *will* or *won't* do. The confusion between will and will not is a reflection of his tortured state of mind.
- ◎ Would it have been different if the first word had been 'No', instead of 'Not'? 'Not' is probably stronger, more definite.
- ◎ How positive is line 4?

Lines 5–8

◎   Read on: what introduces the contrast between the first section and this one? The little word 'But' is the first contrasting linker. Is 'thou' the same addressee as in line 1, 'Despair'?

◎   Its features are presented very alliteratively through these four lines: which expressions do you find particularly forceful? What do the exclamations 'ah', 'O', and 'O' add to the text, for you?

◎   What kind of suffering is this, do you think — physical, mental, spiritual, or a combination of these? What *physical* suggestions do you find in the words?

◎   The end of the octet, line 8, has moved on from 'not feast on thee' (line 1) to 'frantic to avoid thee and flee'. How much has 'I' actually progressed, in your opinion?

Lines 9–14

◎   What is 'Why?' (line 9) asking? It repeats the 'why' of line 5 but the answer perhaps begins to change in line 12.

◎   Find the contrasts with 'toil' and 'coil' (line 10) in line 11.

◎   '… since … I kissed the rod,/ Hand rather' (lines 10–11) is probably religious in its connotations: relating to lines 12 and 14. 'I' also relates with his 'hero' (line 12).

◎   The final lines bring together many of the binaries of the whole text: me/him; attraction/repulsion; toil and coil/strength and joy; feast/flee; comfort/despair … The movement between the first line and the last line could be seen as a move from anger at his despair to a finding of comfort.

Does it help you to know that the poet was expressing, in his so-called 'terrible' sonnets, something of his religious anguish as a priest? Do you need to share his religious feelings in order to appreciate the torment he describes?

Read the poem again, trying to bring out the twisting and turning of emotions and reactions, as he lies wrestling with his despair, his emotions, his (my God!) God. Does it reach any conclusion, or any peace?

Gerard Manley Hopkins used what he called **sprung rhythm** to allow himself greater flexibility with his poetic lines, beyond the traditional syllable count. He also invents words (like the adjective 'wring-world' in line 6), twists syntax, uses repetitions and exclamations; but he does not lose rhyme, and keeps strictly to the fourteen-line form of the sonnet. Trace the rhyme scheme and the sonnet structure.

Activity

Compare the tortured language of 'Carrion Comfort' with the balance and order of Text: Poem (iii). How similar are the themes?

Text: Poem (iii)

(iii)   I find no peace and all my war is done;
I fear and hope, I burn and freeze like ice;
I fly above the wind, yet can I not arise,
And naught I have and all the world I seize on;
5   That looseth nor locketh holdeth me in prison,
And holdeth me not yet can I scape nowise;
Nor letteth me live nor die at my devise,
And yet of death it giveth none occasion.
Without eyen I see, and without tongue I plain;
10   I desire to perish, and yet I ask health;
I love another, and thus I hate myself;
I feed me in sorrow, and laugh in all my pain.
Likewise displeaseth me both death and life,
And my delight is causer of this strife.

◎   Do binaries and contrasts emerge easily? List some. Is there a balance, comparing the first line and the last line?

◎   What is the heart of his problem? Or does he not tell us?

◎   How emotional do you find this poem, compared with 'Carrion Comfort'?

◎   Trace the rhyme scheme and sonnet structure. Do they help the sense?

Commentary

This was one of the very earliest sonnets in English, and is an almost direct translation of an Italian sonnet by Petrarch. You might like to compare it with one or two others – from Shakespeare, to Shelley, and on to Hopkins – to see some of the ways in which the sonnet developed from this Petrarchan model.

The emotions are carefully balanced throughout: from 'peace' and 'war' in the very first line it is clear that the sonnet is playing with balance, just as the earlier Hopkins sonnet plays with tortured, twisted emotions and doubts reflected in tortured, twisted syntax and images.

It is interesting that there is no particular movement or progress by the end of the sonnet – it simply confirms, with examples, the statement of the first line without real changes or developments.

Activity

In Text: Poem (iv), again by Hopkins, look for the initial negative emotions; then see if you notice where any changes or developments emerge.

Text: Poem (iv)

> (**iv**)   No worst, there is none. Pitched past pitch of grief,
>   More pangs will, schooled at forepangs, wilder wring.
>   Comforter, where, where is your comforting?
>   Mary, mother of us, where is your relief?
>   5 My cries heave, herds-long; huddle in a main, a chief
>   Woe, world-sorrow; on an age-old anvil wince and sing –
>   Then lull, then leave off. Fury had shrieked 'No ling-
>   ering! Let me be fell: force I must be brief.'
>   O the mind, mind has mountains; cliffs of fall
> 10 Frightful, sheer, no-man-fathomed. Hold them cheap
>   May who ne'er hung there. Nor does long our small
>   Durance deal with that steep or deep. Here! creep,
>   Wretch, under a comfort serves in a whirlwind: all
>   Life death does end and each day dies with sleep.

Commentary

1   As with 'Carrion Comfort', this text makes a deliberate use of complex word order to express a state of mind. The complexity of these lines could be made simpler in rewritten versions. You might want to try different versions to see what happens, with lines 10–12 in particular.

2   Line divisions contribute to the uncertainty of the words, by holding the reader up; at line 7, and on the cliffs, for example (line

9), and changing the usual word order in the next line.

3   What religious references do you find?

4   Some lines have the regular ten syllables, others do not. Trace the line lengths, the rhyme scheme, and the sonnet structure. Do you think there may be reasons for the more regular lines here than we found in 'Carrion Comfort'?

5   There are similarities between this and 'Carrion Comfort': look for similar words, alliterations, and original inventions. Is the subject the same? What specific binaries are there? And what specific emotions are mentioned? Is this more 'world-sorrow' (line 6) than personal anguish, in your opinion? Or is it both?

All the questions about these three sonnets (poems ii–iv) should bring out something of the shared ideas, but different approaches. 'Carrion Comfort' is the most tortured, 'I Find No Peace' the most balanced and controlled, 'No Worst' the most dizzying, perhaps because of these cliffs! The subject matter is very negative in the first, where the vocabulary, the endless questions, and the fractured syntax emphasise despair and personal pain, although trying to reject despair. The second tries to be more rational; its paradoxes are simple (love/ hate, etc.), its conclusion an echo of the first line. 'No Worst' actually moves all the way through, towards comfort and sleep.

◎   In Shakespeare's *King Lear*, Edgar says, 'The worst is not, / So long as we can say, "This is the worst." ' How close is that to what Hopkins is saying?

◎   Compared with Sir Thomas Wyatt's 'I Find No Peace', the two Hopkins sonnets use a wide range of imagery: pick out some, and compare their use with the simpler images (like 'burn' and 'freeze' – line 2) used by Wyatt.

◎   Make some notes which help you to compare and to contrast the four sonnets in this unit. You could refer to such things as length of lines, shape, rhyme, the voice and who it is addressing, vocabulary, syntax and sentence structure, contrasts and binaries, time: all of these, before even mentioning the themes.

We have seen that it can be illuminating to compare the beginning and the end of a text. It shows there has been movement, often even as simple as a movement of the tense of the verb from past to present (as in 'The Fly', in Unit 2).

We will now look at two very well-known texts, bringing together this idea of movement and what we have seen about syntax.

Activity

As you read Text: Poem (v), pick out as many *positive* words as possible.

Text: Poem (v)

(v)   I wandered lonely as a cloud
       That floats on high o'er vales and hills,
       When all at once I saw a crowd,
       A host of golden daffodils;
   5   Beside the lake, beneath the trees,
       Fluttering and dancing in the breeze.

       Continuous as the stars that shine
       And twinkle on the milky way,
       They stretched in never-ending line
  10   Along the margin of a bay:
       Ten thousand saw I at a glance,
       Tossing their heads in sprightly dance.

       The waves beside them danced; but they
       Out-did the sparkling waves in glee:
  15   A poet could not but be gay,
       In such a jocund company:
       I gazed – and gazed – but little thought
       What wealth the show to me had brought:

       For oft, when on my couch I lie
  20   In vacant or in pensive mood,
       They flash upon that inward eye
       Which is the bliss of solitude;
       And then my heart with pleasure fills,
       And dances with the daffodils.

◎   Was the word 'lonely' (line 1) among your choice of possible words?
    How does it relate to 'the bliss of solitude' (line 22)?
◎   Are there any other binaries apart from *positive* and *negative*?
◎   What does 'I' do in the poem? What does 'I' *not* do in line 17?
◎   How many daffodils did he see (line 11)? '. . . at a glance'?! Is this for
    real?

◎   What are 'They' (line 9) and 'them' (line 13)?

◎   Line 15 presents some problems: is 'A poet' the same as 'I'? Is he gay? How does 'gay' relate to 'jocund' (line 16)?

Commentary

1   If you blanked out the word 'daffodils', would the poem still be about flowers? Read it again, and see what else they could be. Words like 'Fluttering and dancing' (line 6) and 'Tossing their heads' (line 12) might make you think of birds — is that a possible reading?

2   'Could not but' is a nice example of positive/negative occurring in the syntax at the same time. Part of the movement of the whole poem is between negative ('lonely') and positive ('the bliss of solitude'). And 'I' has become third-person, making a subjective/objective binary.

3   The verb tenses in the final stanza move from past to present, and 'For' (line 19) links the previous line to the final stanza, by explaining the 'little thought' (line 17).

4   'Vacant' and 'pensive' (line 20) seem similar, but are in fact different — indeed, opposites (binaries again).

5   Now check the beginning/end contrasts: there is a movement from 'I' (line 1) to 'my heart' (line 23); first-person subject to third-person; 'wandered' (past tense, line 1) to 'dances' (present tense, line 24) — also a different kind of movement. Consider also the movement between some other words: 'lonely' and 'with', 'as' (implying similarity but distance) and 'with', 'a cloud' (in the air) and 'daffodils' (on the ground). Also, in the final stanza, the poet is lying down — horizontal, where he was presumably vertical as he 'wandered'.

6   Perhaps, however, the most significant movement is seen at line 19. Until this point, who has been the subject of the poem? It is all 'I': subject — verb — object (I — see — daffodils).

At line 11, this becomes 'Ten thousand saw I . . .' — 'I' is still the subject, but the daffodils take the emphatic position; 'I' the less important one. 'I' even becomes third person in line 15.

From line 19, 'I' is lying down — passive, acted upon rather than active. The daffodils become the subject: 'They flash . . .' (line 21). And 'I' is no more. For 'then' (line 23) (which indicates more movement of time — as we saw in 'The Fly' and 'When I Have Fears') the subject becomes 'my heart': this is a move from outside to inside, external perception to internal reaction. The binaries accumulate!

7   One thing that is *not* mentioned is memory. He does not *actively* remember the daffodils — 'They flash' (line 21). He does not say 'I remember/recollect the daffodils.' The movement is *not* from experience to recall, but from active to passive, outward to inward. It is not, despite some critics, 'emotion recollected in tranquillity'.

8   *Patterns* of language use are important: rhyme is an obvious form of patterning. There are many other kinds, especially lexical patterning, the way words are grouped together, repeated, varied, and manipulated. A grammatical pattern of *subject − verb − object* could be given, then varied, then returned to, for instance. 'Daffodils' shows examples of both of these, lexical and grammatical patterning. Conjunctions can be used to head each section of a text, like 'When ... When ... When ...' in 'When I Have Fears'; and an absence of pattern could be equally significant − just as what *isn't* said is as important as what is said. Rewriting 'This Is Just to Say' imposed a pattern on a lack of pattern.

Activity

In Text: Poem (vi), how many voices do you find?

Text: Poem (vi)

(vi)   I met a traveller from an antique land
        Who said: Two vast and trunkless legs of stone
        Stand in the desert ... Near them, on the sand,
        Half sunk, a shattered visage lies, whose frown,
    5   And wrinkled lip, and sneer of cold command,
        Tell that its sculptor well those passions read
        Which yet survive, stamped on these lifeless things,
        The hand that mocked them, and the heart that fed:
        And on the pedestal these words appear:
    10 'My name is Ozymandias, king of kings:
        Look on my works, ye Mighty, and despair!'
        Nothing beside remains. Round the decay
        Of that colossal wreck, boundless and bare
        The lone and level sands stretch far away.

Whose voice says the last three lines – 'I' or the 'traveller'? Or can we not tell?

Commentary

1 If we do a first line/last line comparison, what movement emerges?
   Movement from: 'I' and 'a traveller' to ....
                         active verb 'met' to ....
                         past tense to ....
                         'an antique land' to ....
                         the voice of 'I' to ....

So, even before looking closely at the text, we can see there has been a fair amount of movement in terms of person, time, setting, and voice. What we can now look at is how these relate to the rest of the text.

2 What do 'boundless and bare' (line 13) refer to? How do they relate to lines 2 and 3? Put together the pieces of the 'wreck' in lines 2–5. How complete is the picture they make?

   The answer is not very complete: it is a hotch-potch of bits and pieces; more an 'impressionistic' picture than a complete face – underlining the idea of fragmentation.

3 What did the sculptor 'read well'? Does the **internal rhyme** help the sense here, or just help the sound, in your opinion?

4 Line 8 is a bit of a problem in terms of syntax. Does it follow 'read' (i.e. 'the sculptor ... read ... The hand ...') or 'survive' (i.e. 'those passions ... survive ... The hand ...'), or does it relate to 'these lifeless things' (i.e. 'The hand' is among the lifeless things)?

   There could be several ways of exploring this. What is exciting is that, in a poem about fragments and loss, the poet, precisely at the end of the octet, allows the syntax to fragment too – just before coming to the strongest assertion of all, the words on the pedestal (which are themselves a fragment); most probably they are 'spoken' by Ozymandias himself, but he is, of course, no longer present. They may be the sculptor's words too. In some ways, there is a presence/ absence binary here: how much does it connect with ideas of presence and absence throughout the poem?

5 Fragments and details, minute detail and empty desolation, 'vast' remains but without the main substance of the trunk, 'Mighty'/ 'despair', all emerge as contrasts. Some critics have described these contrasts as ironic. Do you like that word to describe the poem? For

you, is it more about power, or loss, or the passing of time, the lasting power of art, all of these – or what?

6   Is the final image of emptiness similar in any way to the last line of 'When I Have Fears'? It could also be contrasted with the final lines of 'Dover Beach' (Poetry Project, pp. 124–25): these images of 'waste lands' anticipating similar ideas of desolation in twentieth-century writing.

Extension

It might be time now to start listing some of the ways we have found to compare texts and bring out contrasts between them. Choose two or three texts from among the ones you have read and simply list the kinds of things that you could tell someone who wanted you to show them how they work differently.

Do a sales pitch for one of the texts you think works particularly well: you are trying to convince someone who doesn't actually think it's worth reading!

Sources

(i) John Keats, 'When I Have Fears' (1818); (ii) Gerard Manley Hopkins, 'Carrion Comfort' (c. 1885); (iii) Thomas Wyatt, 'I Find No Peace' (c. 1540); (iv) Gerard Manley Hopkins, 'No Worst' (c. 1885); (v) William Wordsworth, 'Daffodils' (1804/15); (vi) Percy Bysshe Shelley, 'Ozymandias' (1818)

The appeal

There has always been popular poetry - from ballads, and stories in epic form, through to music-hall and pop songs. Since critics started writing about poetry, there has also been the upmarket view of poetry, leading to the 'canon' of what is considered great. Even before that, though, there was 'private' poetry, written for circulation among a small group of readers, with no wider ambitions. Shakespeare's sonnets were first circulated in this way.

Activity

We are going to look at some contrasting *popular* (**low-culture?**) and **high-culture** poems (Text: Poems (i)–(x)). Look quickly at a few lines of all of them, or of three or four at a time (i)–(iii) and (iv)–(vi) go together, for instance). What does the language tell you about them? Which of them sound to you as if they would have been popular?

Text: Poem (i)

(i)   'O where have you been, Lord Randal my son?
And where have you been, my handsome young man?'
'I have been at the greenwood; mother, make my bed soon,
For I'm wearied with hunting and fain would lie down.'

5   'And who met you there, Lord Randal my son?
And who met you there, my handsome young man?'
'O I met with my true love; mother, make my bed soon,
For I'm wearied with hunting and fain would lie down.'

'And what did she give you, Lord Randal my son?
10   And what did she give you, my handsome young man?'
'Eels fried in a pan; mother, make my bed soon,
For I'm wearied with hunting and fain would lie down.'

'And who got your leavings, Lord Randal my son?
And who got your leavings, my handsome young man?'
15   'My hawks and my hounds; mother, make my bed soon,
For I'm wearied with hunting and fain would lie down.'

'And what became of them, Lord Randal my son?
And what became of them, my handsome young man?'
'They stretched their legs out and died; mother, make my bed
   soon,
20   For I'm wearied with hunting and fain would lie down.'

'O I fear you are poisoned, Lord Randal my son,
I fear you are poisoned, my handsome young man.'
'O yes, I am poisoned; mother, make my bed soon,
For I'm sick at the heart and fain would lie down.'

Can you distil the 'story' into a sentence? So, what do the repetitions and the question/answer form add to that basic story?

If you check out the Bob Dylan song 'A Hard Rain's A-Gonna Fall', you will find that he steals the first two lines of 'Lord Randal'. You might like to think about why he did that, and the use he made of them.

Text: Poem (ii)

(ii)   Who would true valour see,
Let him come hither;
One here will constant be,
Come wind, come weather.

5 There's no discouragement
Shall make him once relent
His first avow'd intent
To be a pilgrim.

◎   What can you tell from the verse forms and rhymes?

◎   If you already know this text, how does that influence your response to it?

◎   What do the concepts of 'true valour' (line 1) and 'pilgrim' (line 8) convey to you?

Text: Poem (iii)

(iii)   Should auld acquaintance be forgot
And never brought to mind?
Should auld acquaintance be forgot
And auld lang syne?

5 For auld lang syne, my jo,
For auld lang syne,
We'll tak' a cup o' kindness yet,
For auld lang syne.

This is probably universally the most familiar poem of all – but how many people know the words, or even what the last line means? ('For [the sake of] old [times] long ago'; 'syne' = 'since'.)

The poet Robert Burns, as he often did, used an old tune and put new words to it.

By the way, is there an answer to the question in the first line?

Text: Poem (iv)

(iv)   Methought I saw how wealthy men
Did grind the poor men's faces,
And greedily did prey on them,
Not pitying their cases;
5 They make them toil and labour sore
For wages too, too small;
The rich men in the tavern roar,
But poor men pay for all. [...]

Methought I met, sore discontent,
10 Some poor men on the way;
I askèd one whither he went
So fast and could not stay.
Quoth he, 'I must go take my lease,
Or else another shall;
15 My landlord's riches do increase,
But poor men pay for all.' [...]

Methought I was in the country,
Where poor men take great pains
And labour hard continually
20 Only for rich men's gains:
Like th' Israelites in Egypt,
The poor are kept in thrall;
The task-masters are playing kept,
But poor men pay for all.

Which of the following does Text: Poem (iv) contain: pain, anger, suffering, subjectivity, objectivity, humour, acceptance? When might it have been written? How can you tell?

Text: Poem (v)

(v)   With fingers weary and worn,
      With eyelids heavy and red,
      A Woman sat, in unwomanly rags,
      Plying her needle and thread –
5   Stitch! stitch! stitch!
      In poverty, hunger, and dirt,
      And still with a voice of dolorous pitch
      She sang the 'Song of the Shirt!'
      'Work! work! work!
10   While the cock is crowing aloof!
      And work – work – work,
      Till the stars shine through the roof!'

◎ What effect do you think is meant here – sympathy for the woman (or do you find it patronising?), anger at the exploitation of such workers, or what?

◎ Is it similar in its effect to 'Poor Men Pay for All', or do you react in a different way? Examine how the texts are similar or different, and how reactions to them might vary.

◎ In what period do you think 'The Song of the Shirt' might have been written? Does it show any political commitment, or does it merely describe, in your opinion?

Text: Poem (vi)

(vi)   [...] I paint the Cot,
      As Truth will paint it, and as Bards will not:
      Nor you, ye poor, of lettered scorn complain,
      To you the smoothest song is smooth in vain;
5   O'ercome by labour, and bowed down by time,
      Feel you the barren flattery of a rhyme?
      Can poets soothe you, when you pine for bread,
      By winding myrtles round your ruined shed?

◎ This is clearly not a ballad – how can you tell? What does it have in common with the previous two texts? What is 'the Cot' (line 1)?

◎ How does 'I' see himself, in contrast with 'Bards' (line 2)?

◎ Lines 4–7 could be interpreted as referring to the previous text, Thomas Hood's 'The Song of the Shirt'. Do you think that is the sort of thing 'I' might have been referring to?

Text: Poem (vii)

(vii)　Here with a Loaf of Bread beneath the Bough,
A Flask of Wine, a Book of Verse - and Thou
Beside me singing in the Wilderness -
And Wilderness is Paradise enow. [. . .]

5　The Moving Finger writes; and having writ,
Moves on: nor all thy Piety nor Wit
Shall lure it back to cancel half a Line,
Nor all thy Tears wash out a Word of it.

And that inverted Bowl we call The Sky,
10　Whereunder crawling coop't we live and die,
Lift not thy hands to It for help - for It
Rolls impotently on as Thou or I.

With Earth's first Clay They did the Last Man's knead,
And then of the Last Harvest sow'd the Seed:
15　Yea, the first Morning of Creation wrote
What the Last Dawn of Reckoning shall read.

◎ This text, from The Rubaiyat of Omar Khayyam, is full of 'quotes' – famous lines that have become part of the language. Are there any lines you particularly like?

◎ Do you find the tone different from others in this unit?

◎ Do past, present, and future figure in this text too?

Text: Poem (viii)

(viii)   If you can keep your head when all about you
Are losing theirs and blaming it on you,
If you can trust yourself when all men doubt you,
But make allowance for their doubting too;

5   If you can wait and not be tired by waiting,
Or being lied about, don't deal in lies,
Or being hated, don't give way to hating,
And yet don't look too good, nor talk too wise:

If you can dream – and not make dreams your master;
10   If you can think – and not make thoughts your aim;
If you can meet with Triumph and Disaster
And treat those two impostors just the same. [. . .]

If you can fill the unforgiving minute
With sixty seconds' worth of distance run,
15   Yours is the Earth and everything that's in it,
And – which is more – you'll be a Man, my son!

◎   This might *seem* less rhythmic than some other texts, but check out the rhyme scheme and line length, and see what you find.

◎   What kind of values does *If* put forward? Do you find them out-of-date, worth thinking about, superficial, valid, or what?

◎   Are there any lines you find particularly striking? Why? What about the final line?

Text: Poem (ix)

(ix)   I wonder by my troth, what thou, and I
Did, till we lov'd? Were we not weaned till then?
But suck'd on country pleasures, childishly?
Or snorted we in the seven sleepers' den?
5   'Twas so; But this, all pleasures fancies be,
If ever any beauty I did see,
Which I desir'd, and got, 'twas but a dream of thee.

And now good morrow to our waking souls,
Which watch not one another out of fear;
10   For love, all love of other sights controls,
And makes one little room, an every where.
Let sea-discovers to new worlds have gone,
Let Maps to others, worlds on worlds have shown,
Let us possess one world, each hath one, and is one.

15   My face in thine eye, thine in mine appears,
And true plain hearts do in the faces rest,
Where can we find two better hemispheres
Without sharp North, without declining West?
What ever dies, was not mixt equally;
20   If our two loves be one, or thou and I
Love so alike, that none do slacken, none can die.

◎   The first stanza opens with questions, not all of them immediately clear in their references: where are the questions answered? How do the questions tie in with the last three lines of the stanza?

◎   Is 'But' (line 5) a simple connector, or does it mean 'beside'?

◎   What is 'this' (line 5)?

◎   The first line of the second stanza contains the poem's title, '[The] Good Morrow'. Are there two levels of 'waking' (line 8)?

◎   Where does the stanza move out from the limited, personal world of the lovers? What other binaries like this (microcosm/macrocosm; 'little room'/'every where' – line 11) can you find through the whole poem? How are past, present, and future linked?

◎   What kinds of exploration does 'I' mention – geographical and personal?

◎ In line 15, how do they actually see each other's faces?

◎ How do they know their love will not die, according to line 19?

◎ Check out the rhyme scheme and line lengths. Do you think the extra syllables in the last line of each stanza are possibly an *adding on*, to underline the thematic ideas of the poem?

◎ Line 4 is probably obscure: how much do we *need* clarification, in order to get something out of the poem as a whole? ('The seven sleepers' den' is a reference to a Greek legend of seven young men of Ephesus who took refuge in a cave to avoid persecution, and survived there for over two centuries – a kind of early Rip van Winkle story!) The idea is of a state of innocence or unworldliness, before the new beginning (the 'good morrow' of line 8), that the love relationship brought.

◎ Line 3 suggests another parallel state of innocence – also pagan – in a sort of country Arcadia or Paradise; and line 2 suggests 'we' were babies, 'till we lov'd'. Before Milton (see Unit 1, p. 8), the poet John Donne gives the idea that loss of innocence is necessary to enjoy love.

Text: Poem (x)

(**x**)   I struck the board, and cried, 'No more!
               I will abroad.
      What? shall I ever sigh and pine?
My lines and life are free; free as the road,
5   Loose as the wind, as large as store.
        Shall I be still in suit?
    Have I no harvest but a thorn
    To let me blood, and not restore
    What I have lost with cordial fruit?
10   Sure there was wine
Before my sighs did dry it: there was corn
        Before my tears did drown it.
    Is the year only lost to me?
        Have I no bays to crown it?
15 No flowers, no garlands gay? all blasted?
          All wasted?
    Not so, my heart: but there is fruit,
        And thou hast hands.
    Recover all thy sigh-blown age

```
20    On double pleasures: leave thy cold dispute
       Of what is fit, and not. Forsake thy cage,
                              Thy rope of sands,
       Which petty thoughts have made, and made to thee
          Good cable, to enforce and draw,
25                              And be thy law,
          While thou didst wink and wouldst not see.
                         Away; take heed:
                         I will abroad.
       Call in thy death's head there: tie up thy fears.
30                         He that forbears
             To suit and serve his need,
                         Deserves his load.'
       But as I raved and grew more fierce and wild
                         At every word,
35           Methoughts I heard one calling, 'Child!'
             And I replied, 'My Lord.'
```

◎ In terms of form, and line length, this is highly adventurous. Check out where the short lines contain a complete question or statement: do they reinforce the words, by being short? Are any lines repeated exactly?

◎ What about the rhymes, and the overall rhyme scheme? Are there any half rhymes or **eye rhymes**?

◎ What binaries and contrasts can you find − freedom/confinement is the main one. Others might include line 31: what do you think the contrast between 'suit and serve [his need]' means?

◎ What lines give an idea of wasted time?

◎ Who is 'thou' in line 18?

◎ Check out verb tenses − between present, past, and present perfect. What do they tell you about 'I' 's state of mind?

◎ 'I' asks a lot of questions. Where does he answer the questions posed in line 3, lines 7−9, lines 13−16? He also uses a lot of imperatives. Who is he talking to with these, for example, in lines 19−21, lines 27−29?

The title of this poem is 'The Collar'. Like Gerard Manley Hopkins, the poet George Herbert was a man of the church who wrestled with his faith. How much do you see 'The Collar' as a religious text, and how much

48

could it be read as about any internal conflict?

Some images might seem a bit puzzling at first: examine any of them you find interesting, and decide what they mean *for you*.

What does a comparison of the first and last lines show?

From the ten poems in this unit, what makes you choose some as popular – the rhythm, the sounds, the words? Are the ones you decided were popular more simple or more complex, in general?

Commentary

What should emerge from these ten texts is a range of roles for poetry: 'Lord Randal' tells an old folk tale in question-and-answer dialogue form, between mother and son. The story of the fatal meeting with 'my true love' is surprisingly close to 'La Belle Dame sans Merci' (p. 83–84).

(ii) has become well known as a hymn. It extols religious virtues, which 'If' (viii) in some ways echoes, but the verse forms are quite different. If you know the tune, you can contrast this with the tune of (iii): more downbeat, nostalgic, where the hymn tune is upbeat, martial. If there is an answer to the question about 'auld acquaintance', it might be in line 7, meaning we won't forget it.

Text (iv) shows a different kind of concern – more social than individual. There is anger and suffering, viewed very subjectively through the eyes of the speaker. It was written in the 1640s, but could have been written at any time in history. The next two texts continue this idea of social outrage, but 'The Song of the Shirt' is not quite so directly involving: it is a third-person description rather than a first-person view, so might have a slightly different impact on the reader. The language of (iv) is a little bit more archaic ('Quoth he', etc.) than the woman's song, but otherwise they could easily be from any period. Text (vi) talks about this kind of 'song' – what the poet is doing here is complaining about the way some poets glorify poverty. This is the idea of 'winding myrtles' in the last line. For him, 'the Cot' (the poor people's cottage) is to be seen realistically rather than 'as Bards' 'paint it'. But isn't there a contradiction in his saying this in carefully rhymed pentameter? A ballad would have had a different form – four-line stanzas with quite a lot of repetition, probably.

Text (vii) takes us on to another level entirely. Lines 2 and 5–6 are probably the best known. It is full of assertions in the present simple tense: these pass for simple worldly wisdom, easy to digest and memorable, which might account for some of the poem's appeal. It also

49

panders to the mid-Victorian taste for the slightly 'oriental' – an escape from the realities of 'The Song of the Shirt'. Text (viii) is almost the opposite: the 'Manly' strengths of the British Empire, rather than the hedonism of 'A Flask of Wine' and the idea of just letting time pass. Here time has to be put to constructive use (as in lines 13–14). The two texts show quite contrasting philosophies of life. *If* sets up balances – 'if . . .' 'and . . .' – but never asks 'if not'? Both are very carefully and rhythmically structured: the first in ten-syllable lines with a clear rhyme scheme, the second using eleven-syllable lines alternately with ten-syllable lines, and regular rhymes.

The final two texts are quite different from the rest, and will take more working out: hence the greater number of questions. It is characteristic of the so-called **metaphysical** poets of the seventeenth century to give the readers quite a lot to do. Where the earlier texts in this unit used simple language and forms, (ix) and (x) have a degree of complexity which might initially put some people off – but they reward attention.

In (ix), line 5 answers the early questions: the two lovers did not really exist till they loved. 'But' (line 5) means 'apart from' this experience of love; all the beauty 'I' saw before this was nothing compared to 'thee'. The sun wakes the lovers, and reawakens the love in their souls; in line 11, their room becomes a universe. This leads to the metaphysical **conceit** of exploration of the whole world. (The poem was written at the time when voyages of exploration were opening up whole new worlds.) Binaries such as 'one world'/'others' emerge, while the two lovers become one. Line 15 shows the lovers' eyes reflecting each other, and the whole stanza goes on to stress equality, denying geographical distance and even denying mortality. Despite the obscure references and conceits, the overall impression is of a very personal and direct love poem, combining, as Donne often does, passion and intellect.

'The Collar' (x) is more complex: even the layout looks more tortured, with the varying line-lengths (many of only four syllables) questioning and debating the bonds and ties of faith. Among the rhymes: 'abroad'/'road' (lines 2, 4) is an **eye-rhyme** today (although it probably rhymed in the seventeenth century); 'blasted'/'wasted' (lines 15, 16) also, and 'fears'/'forbears' (lines 29, 30). Even the final rhyme, ''word'/'Lord' (lines 34, 36) is not complete, which is perhaps appropriate given the overall tone of uncertainty.

Binaries include 'let'/'restore' (line 8), 'wine'/'dry' (lines 10, 11), 'corn'/'drown' and 'dry'/'drown' (both lines 11, 12), mostly tied in with the idea of freedom/confinement. The word 'lost' is repeated, and lines 13 and 19 suggest the notion of time which might have been wasted, as the flowers and garlands were. Present and past are closely linked throughout, as 'I' wrestles with his present distress and lack of future. But he is constantly answering his own questions (he is 'thou') and offering himself alternatives (line 4, in effect, answers line 3; line 17 answers lines 13–16, and so on), giving himself instructions (lines 19–21, 27–29) until the final intervention of another voice in line 35. By the last line, he has moved from rebellion to acceptance.

Of course, tastes change, and what was once popular can go out of fashion very quickly. Or something which was relatively unknown can suddenly reach a wide audience. Poets like John Donne ('The Good Morrow') and George Herbert ('The Collar') were championed as Metaphysical Poets in the 1920s, by the modern poet and critic T.S. Eliot. As a result, they became highly appreciated in the more intellectual level of poetic popularity, although they had been almost unread for nearly 200 years till then.

The Rubaiyat of Omar Khayyam, in an English version by Edward Fitzgerald, was one of the most popular of all poems for over a century. It derives from a twelfth-century Persian poem, but is liberally reinterpreted rather than being a direct translation. Kipling's 'If' has been popular for almost a century, since it was first published. In a recent BBC radio poll, it was named as the best-loved poem by more listeners than any other: this maybe tells us more about listeners to BBC radio than about poetry! Other top favourites included William Wordsworth's 'Daffodils' (in Unit 3) and Stevie Smith's 'Not Waving But Drowning' (in Unit 8).

Extension

Make a list of some of your top favourite songs, poems or quotes. Some of them will be well known and some maybe not. It will be interesting to see if there is any way they divide into 'high culture' and 'low culture' – these are very subjective classifications anyway. But do some of them have a different kind of appeal from others? If so, the question arises, what is it that makes the appeal different? The same thing happens with any questions of taste: Mozart is different from Madonna. Sometimes it only depends in the mood you are in when you read or hear something, or on how it was first presented to you.

See if you can set down some of your own reasons why some texts appeal to you – and maybe even why some don't.

51

Sources

(i) Anonymous, 'Lord Randal' (15th century); (ii) John Bunyan, extract from 'To Be a Pilgrim' (1678); (iii) Robert Burns, extract from 'Auld Lang Syne' (1786); (iv) Anonymous, 'Poor Men Pay for All' (1640s); (v) Thomas Hood, 'extract from The Song of the Shirt' (1843); (vi) George Crabbe, extract from 'The Village' (1783) (vii) Edward Fitzgerald, extract from *The Rubaiyat of Omar Khayyam* (1859); (viii) Rudyard Kipling, extract from 'If' (1910); (ix) John Donne, 'The Good Morrow' (*c.* 1600); (x) George Herbert, 'The Collar' (1620s).

The places

We have already looked at some 'voices' in poems. But voices can also represent places, **dialects**, whole societies. In this unit we are going to look at local voices in poetry.

Look quickly through the first twelve texts. Where do think they might have been written? See if you can identify Australian, Scottish, Irish, Jamaican, Indian, Malaysian, American and African voices, as well as a couple of English dialects.

Which look the most difficult to read, at first glance? Which the easiest? What is it that makes the difference?

There are probably some words and phrases in most of them that are unfamiliar. As you read more closely, pick them out and see if you can decide what they mean.

The first poem is a direct cross-reference to a text in Unit 1 — a rewriting into Glasgow dialect. What kind of differences do you notice in what the text says?

Text: Poems (i)-(xii)

(i)   *Just ti Let Yi No*

ahv drank
thi speshlz
that wurrin
thi frij

n thit
yiwurr probbli
hodn back
furthi pahrti

awright
they wur great
that stroang
thaht cawld

(ii)   Yuh hear bout de people dem arres
fi bun dung de Asian people dem house?
Yuh hear bout de policemen dem lock up
fi beat up de black bwoy widout a cause?
Yuh hear bout de M.P. dem sack
because im refuse fi help im black constituents
eena dem fight 'gainst deportation?
Yuh noh hear bout dem?

Me neida.

(iii)   ygUDuh

ydoan
yunnuhstan

ydoan o
yunnustan dem
yguduh ged

yunnustan dem doidee
yguduh ged riduh
ydoan o nudn

LISN bud LISN

dem
gud
am

lidl yelluh bas
tuds weer goin

duhSIVILEYEzum

(iv)   It was a wondrous sight!
A sight for national unity watchers.

He eating fried mee with chopsticks
And she, nasi lemak with fingers.

The young man skilfully
manoeuvred the chopsticks
without letting slip a strand.

The young woman expertly
coordinated her hands and mouth
getting every grain in.

The meal almost over
They make plans to tell their parents.

(v)   Of priests we can offer a charmin' variety,
Far renowned for larnin' and piety;
Still, I'd advance ye widout impropriety,
Father O'Flynn as the flower of them all.

Here's a health to you, Father O'Flynn,
Sláinte, and *sláinte*, and *sláinte* agin;
Powerfulest preacher, and
Tenderest teacher, and
Kindliest creature in ould Donegal.

(vi)   As a African I danced to riddims wild in Nicaragua,
I overstood dem well.
As a African I did not celebrate 200 years of Australia,
I understood its history is black.
As a African I went to find Palestine,
I got confused on de West Bank,
And as a African Palestine is important.

As a African I grew old,
I went and sat down and reasoned with Mr. Ayatollah.
Mr. Ayatollah told me to mind my own business,
and so did Mr. President USA.
Mrs. Thatcher wouldn't even talk to me.

As a African a plastic bullet hit me in Northern Ireland,
But my children overstood an dey grew strong.
As a African I was a woman in a man's world,
A man in a computer world,
A fly on the wall of China,
A Rastafarian diplomat
And a miner in Wales.

I was a red hot Eskimo
A peace loving hippie
A honest newscaster
A city dwelling peasant
I was a Arawak
A unwanted baby
A circumcised lady,
I was all of dis

And still a African.

(**vii**)　Wat a joyful news, Miss Mattie,
I feel like me heart gwine burs
Jamaica people colonizin
Englan in reverse.

By de hundred, by de tousan
From country and from town,
By de ship-load, by de plane-load
Jamaica is Englan boun.

Dem a pour out a Jamaica,
Everybody future plan
Is fe get a big-time job
And settle in de mother lan.

(**viii**)　The springtime it brings on the shearing,
And it's then you will see them in droves,
To the west-country stations all steering,
A-seeking a job off the coves.

Chorus:　With my raggedy old swag on my shoulder
And a billy quart-pot in my hand,
I tell you we'll 'stonish the new chums,
When they see how we travel the land.

From Boonabri up to the border,
Then it's over to Bourke; there and back.
On the hills and the plains you will see them,
The men on the Wallaby Track.

And after the shearing is over
And the wool season's all at an end,
It is then you will see the flash shearers
Making johnny-cakes round in the bend.

(ix)   As I do zew, wi' nimble hand,
         In here avore the window's light,
         How still do all the housegear stand
         Around my lwonesome zight.
         How still do all the housegear stand
         Since Willie now 've a-left the land.

         The rwose-tree's window sheäden bow
         Do hang in leaf, an' win'-blow'd flow'rs
         Avore my lwonesome eyes do show
         Theäse bright November hours.
         Avore my lwonesome eyes do show
         Wi' nwone but I to zee em blow.

                    (x)   Friends,
                           our dear sister
                           is departing for foreign
                           in two three days,
                           and
                           we are meeting today
                           to wish her bon voyage.

                           You are all knowing, friends,
                           what sweetness is in Miss Pushpa.
                           I don't mean only external sweetness
                           but internal sweetness.
                           Miss Pushpa is smiling and smiling
                           even for no reason
                           but simply because she is feeling.

                           Miss Pushpa is coming
                           from very high family.
                           Her father was renowned advocate
                           In Bulsar or Surat,
                           I am not remembering now which place.

                           Surat? Ah, yes,
                           once only I stayed in Surat
                           with family members
                           of my uncle's very old friend,
                           his wife was cooking nicely . . .
                           that was long time ago.

                           Coming back to Miss Pushpa
                           she is most popular lady
                           with men also and ladies also.

57

Whenever I asked her to do anything,
she was saying, 'Just now only
I will do it.' That is showing
good spirit. I am always
appreciating the good spirit.
Pushpa Miss is never saying no.
Whatever I or anybody is asking
she is always saying yes,
and today she is going
to improve her prospect,
and we are wishing her bon voyage.

Now I ask other speakers to speak,
and afterwards Miss Pushpa
will do summing up.

(xi)   Me an' thy muther, Sammy, 'as beän a-talkin' o' thee;
Thou's been talkin' to muther, an' she beän a tellin' it me.
Thou'll not marry for munny – thou's sweet upo' parson's lass –
Noä – thou'll marry for luvv – an' we boäth on us thinks tha an
    ass.

Seeäd her todaäy goä by – Saäint's-daäy – they was ringing the
    bells.
She's a beauty thou thinks – an' soä is scoors o' gells,
Them as 'as munny an' all – wot's a beauty? – the flower as blaws.
But proputty, proputty sticks, an' proputty, proputty graws.

Do'ant be stunt: taäke time: I knaws what maäkes tha sa mad.
Warn't I craäzed fur the lasses mysén when I wur a lad?

(xii)   Wee, sleekit, cowrin, tim'rous beastie,
    O, what a panic's in thy breastie!
    Thou need na start awa sae hasty
        Wi' bickering brattle!
    I wad be laith to rin an' chase thee,
        Wi' murdering pattle!

I'm truly sorry man's dominion
Has broken Nature's social union,
An' justifies that ill opinion
    Which makes thee startle
At me, thy poor, earth-born companion
    An' fellow mortal!

I doubt na, whyles, but thou may thieve;
What then? Poor beastie, thou maun live!
A daimen icker in a thrave
            'S a sma' request;
I'll get a blessin wi' the lave,
            An' never miss't!

Thy wee-bit housie, too, in ruin!
Its silly wa's the win's are strewin!
An' naething, now, to big a new ane,
            O' foggage green!
An' bleak December's win's ensuin,
            Baith snell an' keen!

Thou saw the fields laid bare an' waste,
An' weary winter comin fast,
An' cozie here, beneath the blast,
            Thou thought to dwell,
Till crash! the cruel coulter past
            Out thro' thy cell.

That wee bit heap o' leaves an' stibble,
Hast cost thee monie a weary nibble!
Now thou's turned out, for a' thy trouble,
            But house or hald,
To thole the winter's sleety dribble,
            An' cranreuch cauld!

But Mousie, thou art no thy lane,
In proving foresight may be vain:
The best-laid schemes o' mice an' men
            Gang aft agley,
An' lea'e us nought but grief an' pain,
            For promis'd joy!

Still thou art blest, compared wi' me!
The present only toucheth thee:
But och! I backward cast my e'e,
            On prospects drear!
An' forward, tho' I canna see,
            I guess an' fear!

Commentary

Text (i)

What do you think 'speshlz' are? Fruit? Is the tone different from the earlier poem?

Text (ii)

'Yuh' for 'you' is fairly widespread. In 'Yuh Hear Bout', what other pronouns are there?

◎   Have you decoded 'fi bun dung' (line 2)? What **accent** or dialect does it sound like?

◎   Is the tone angry or humorous?

◎   The poet Valerie Bloom was born in Jamaica; she settled in England at the age of 22.
    ('fi bun dung' is 'for burning down'.)

Text (iii)

In 'ygUDuh', the speech forms are deliberately (American) redneck and rough. What do they contrast with? Who does the last line refer to?

The question boils down to 'Who has got to civilise whom?' if you want to rewrite it! The enemy is coloured ('yelluh'); the speaker is not wonderfully coherent at getting his point across, and blames his listener ('bud') who doesn't know anything.

A binary perhaps between civilised and uncivilised?

Text (iv)

This poem represents two of the cultures of multiracial Malaysia, through food: 'fried mee' is noodles (Chinese); 'nasi lemak' is rice (Malay). Notice the adverbs, showing how well each handles the eating. Which of them is of which race, in your opinion?

◎   Will it be easy for the parents to accept, do you think?

◎   Are the first two lines ironic about 'national unity'?

Text (v)

'Father O'Flynn' is Irish. What kind of tone comes through? What do the adjectives and the rhymes tell you? (*Sláinte*, pronounced 'slange', means 'Cheers!')

Text (vi)

'As a African' is not African. The poet, Benjamin Zephaniah, was born in Birmingham (England) and brought up between the UK and Jamaica. ('Arawak' means belonging to the native people of Jamaica, who are not negroes.) So, what does 'African' come to mean here?

How political are these voices, so far? Should poetry be political? Or is this kind of poetry different from the usual?

The assertion of a local accent, dialect, or even language is often considered political. This might not be so important in the first text, which plays on the supposed Glaswegian penchant for drink (Carlsberg Specials); but there is anger in (ii) and (vi), bigotry in (iii), and perhaps a touch of idealism in the picture of racial harmony (Chinese man and Malay woman) symbolised in food in (iv). The rough language of (iii) makes a neat irony against the notion to 'civilise' ('SIVILEYEz') the 'inferiors'. This is similar to the contrasts in 'As a African', where 'African' stands for every marginalised culture all over the world – there has rarely been such a collection of minorities in one single text.

Text (vii)

This poem, by Louise Bennett, is obviously about Jamaican emigration to England. Is it ironic about 'colonizin / Englan in reverse', do you think? Irony, or the possibility of irony, often depends on the reader – as in (vi), it *could* be read ironically. Perhaps here the reversal of usual viewpoints makes the text more clearly ironic.

Text (viii)

This text is Australian: what words and images confirm this?

Text (ix)

The poet William Barnes typically wrote in the dialect of his native Dorset, in southern England. The 'z' sounding for 's', and the 'w' sound before a long 'o' are features here. What other features do you notice?

Again, the subject is leaving home – Willie is the speaker's brother.

Text (x)

'Goodbye Party for Miss Pushpa T.S.' is Indian, written by an Indian – though it seems to be making fun of the speaker. What features of Indian

English can you pick out? What can you tell about the speaker and about Miss Pushpa?

Text (xi)

This is in Lincolnshire dialect (from eastern England), with long vowels. The subject is one of the oldest in the world – what does Sammy want to do? What do his parents want him to do? It might surprise you to find out that this text is by Tennyson – humour not being what he is best known for!

Text (xii)

'To a Mouse' by Robert Burns is probably the best known of the texts in this unit. There are some famous lines (for example 'The best-laid schemes o' mice an' men / Gang aft agley') and the whole situation – the ploughman wrecking the mouse's home with his plough – is classic. Do you find any echo of William Blake's 'The Fly' (in Unit 2)?

Looking also at the form, at the way 'I' speaks to the mouse, the references to time in the final stanza, you begin to see there is quite a lot going on in the text: it takes in man's relationship with nature, binaries such as human/animal, power/vulnerability, particular/general, microcosm/macrocosm and past, present and future. Sympathy and identification with the 'lower' forms of nature might be seen as the keynote.

Mark some of the particularly Scottish expressions. Then read the words either side of them, to see how much is actually clear. Try substituting more familiar words for the ones you don't know ('awry' for 'agley', for example). Whole stanzas are, in fact, in clear English: the second stanza could sum up the whole poem.

(Some phrases: 'bickering brattle' = scrambling clatter; 'A daimen icker in a thrave' = One small ear of corn out of a stack of sheaves; 'silly' = weak, feeble; 'foggage' = moss; 'Baith snell an' keen' = Both biting and sharp; 'coulter' = plough; 'cranreuch' = frost.)

Extension

1   With many of these texts, we have to hear them or read them aloud to get a better idea of the sense. Would you say the dialect obscures the sense of any of them? Are there any where you feel it is deliberately exaggerated? Why might a poet do that?

2   You might want to try rewriting a text or two in more **standard English** – what is gained, or what is lost, in doing that? Does that give you any further ideas on why a writer might choose to write in dialect rather than in a more standard English?

3   What do these local voices tell you about themselves and their concerns? Are they particularly local, or universal? Are they limited in their appeal because of the kind of language they use? Are they better, or less good, than poems you have read in standard English? Or is there the same range and spread of quality you have found with other texts?

4   Which do you like best? Why?

5   Which do you think will be lasting in their effect, and which more ephemeral?

6   The use of dialect is sometimes criticised as being a self-conscious way of asserting social or geographical difference, otherness. This view sees it as a challenge to other forms, other ways of speaking and writing, and often tries to put it down as a byway of literature, not mainstream. You might like to reflect on that in relation to the texts you have read – and to the next one.

Activity

Tony Harrison famously wrote about how an *accent* can make a line of poetry sound different (see Text: Poem (xiii)). The line he is referring to is 'My heart aches, and a drowsy numbness pains / My sense,' from Keats's 'Ode to a Nightingale'. What is he using the standard/ accented binary to underline, do you think?

Text: Poem (xiii)

(xiii)

I

αἰαῖ, ay, ay! . . . stutterer Demosthenes
gob full of pebbles outshouting seas –

4 words only of *mi 'art aches* and . . . 'Mine's broken,
you barbarian, T.W.!' *He* was nicely spoken.
'Can't have our glorious heritage done to death!'

I played the Drunken Porter in *Macbeth*.

'Poetry's the speech of kings. You're one of those
Shakespeare gives the comic bits to: prose!
All poetry (even Cockney Keats?) you see
's been dubbed [ʌs] into RP,
Received Pronunciation, please believe [ʌs]
your speech is in the hands of the Receivers.'

'We say [ʌs] not [uz], T.W.!' That shut my trap.
I doffed my flat a's (as in 'flat cap')
my mouth all stuffed with glottals, great
lumps to hawk up and spit out . . . *E-nun-ci-ate*!

II

So right, yer buggers, then! We'll occupy
your lousy leasehold Poetry.

I chewed up Littererchewer and spat the bones
into the lap of dozing Daniel Jones,
dropped the initials I'd been harried as
and used my *name* and my own voice: [uz] [uz] [uz],
ended sentences with by, with, from,
and spoke the language that I spoke at home.
RIP RP, RIP T.W.
I'm *Tony* Harrison no longer you!

You can tell the Receivers where to go
(and not aspirate it) once you know
Wordsworth's *matter / water* are full rhymes,
[uz] can be loving as well as funny.

My first mention in the *Times*
automatically made Tony Anthony!

64

Commentary

1   The opening words in Greek are repeated in English immediately. Is this about speech, or society, or both? What is the situation, and who are the speakers?

2   Harrison treats the situation with some humour. Do you find any anger? Is there a sense of frustration as well? Probably there is a bit of both, but the anger and embarrassment he felt in school are still there, even though he has gone beyond them.

3   Almost all of the text demands to be read aloud. What other sound binaries emerge, like '*matter/ water*' four lines from the end of the poem ('funny'/'Anthony', for instance)?

4   The main contrast is between 'I', who is the poet himself as a schoolboy, and the teacher who cares so much about speaking properly. That attitude, though it seems out of date now, still holds in some quarters. Daniel Jones (line 4 of section II) was the great authority on pronunciation: hence Harrison's playing with sounds, and the joke on Receivers (in the context of bankruptcy) contrasting with Received, meaning authorised/ accepted.

5   He names three major figures of 'Littererchewer' – Keats probably had a Cockney (London) accent, Shakespeare a Midlands (Warwickshire) accent, and Wordsworth a northern English (Cumberland) accent. This tells us something about the kind of teacher who insists on 'RP, / **Received Pronunciation**' (lines 10-11 of section I). (Look back to lines 3–4.)

6   The text brings together social attitudes, political attitudes, and cultural awareness. How do you think it reflects each of these?
        Can you trace any similar concerns in the other dialect texts you have read?

Extension

Can you find some poetry – modern or old – in a local dialect or a local variety of English? Look around, ask grandparents, check out libraries: you never know what you might find!

    Very often this kind of poetry is remembered, rather than written down. Of course, it need not be old – there are many voices writing from communities whose linguistic origins are not English.

    With any texts you find, check out how they are similar or different to some of the ones in this unit. It will be interesting to see if you find shared themes or forms of language in any of them, and if they have the same kinds of purpose and effects as the ones you have read.

Sources

(i) Tom Leonard, 'Just ti Let Yi No' (1975); (ii) Valerie Bloom, 'Yuh Hear Bout' (1983); (iii) e.e. cummings, 'ygUDuh' (c. 1930); (iv) Malachi Edwin Vethamani, 'It Was a Wondrous Sight' (1991); (v) A.P. Graves, extract from 'Father O'Flynn' (1889); (vi) Benjamin Zephaniah, 'As a African' (1988); (vii) Louise Bennett, 'Colonization in Reverse' (1982); (viii) E.J. Overbury, 'The Springtime It Brings On the Shearing' (late 19th century); (ix) William Barnes, extract from 'Lwonesomeness' (1861); (x) Nissim Ezekiel, 'Goodbye Party for Miss Pushpa T.S.' (1976); (xi) Alfred, Lord Tennyson, extract from 'Northern Farmer, New Style' (1847); (xii) Robert Burns, 'To a Mouse' (1785); (xiii) Tony Harrison, 'Them and [uz]' (1978).

The genders

Look back through the texts so far and try to list the subjects they have talked about. Do any themes emerge clearly?

Can you set them in such categories as:

◎ social
◎ personal
◎ general/universal
◎ particular/individual?

Love and loss, nature, war, religion/faith, are often seen as the major themes of poetry, at least *explicitly*. But *implicitly*, many of the texts we have seen are also negotiating questions of time (past - present - future), identity (I - you - me), coming to terms with something (pain, death, events, etc.). A good poem is rarely about only one thing.

Have the texts so far been mostly

◎ positive or negative
◎ happy or sad
◎ subjective or objective
◎ masculine or feminine?

Would you describe the language of the texts so far as largely realistic or not? William Wordsworth, like many other poets, wanted to use 'the real language of men'. The questions arise, what is real, and does 'men' exclude women? In the canon of Wordsworth's day, women *were* often excluded, although Wordsworth himself advised and helped Charlotte Smith. It is a sad fact that women tended to be the subject of poems for centuries, rather than the voices heard in the texts.

Activity

Is there such a thing as a 'female sensibility'? Or a male one, for that matter? Look back at Gavin Ewart's poem 'Office Friendships' (p. 20); does that strike you as 'male sensibility'? Or is it just that there are subjects we associate more with one gender rather than the other?

Is the subject matter distinctively feminine in the following five texts (Poems (i)–(v))? Pick out one or two which, at a rapid glance, seem to say something particularly *to* or *about* women.

Text: Poem (i)

(i)   Deprived of freedom, health, and ease,
        And rivalled by such things as these,
        This latest effort will I try,
        Or to regain thy heart, or die.
        Soft as I am, I'll make thee see
        I will not brook contempt from thee!

◎   Who do you think 'thee' could be?

Text: Poem (ii)

(ii)   What is't you mean, that I am thus approached?
Dare you to hope that I may be debauched?
For your seducing words the same implies,
In begging pity, with a soft surprise,
For one who loves, and sighs, and almost dies.

In every word and action doth appear
Something I hate and blush to see or hear.
At first your love for vast respect was told,
Till your excess of manners grew too bold,
And did your base, designing thoughts unfold.

◎   Who is speaking here, and to whom, in your opinion?
◎   What does 'the same' (line 3) refer to?

Text: Poem (iii)

(iii)   A wretched woman, pale and breathless, flies,
And, gazing round her, listens to the sound
Of hostile footsteps: – No! they die away --
Nor noise remains, but of the cataract,
Or surly breeze of night, that mutters low
Among the thickets, where she trembling seeks
A temporary shelter – clasping close
To her quick-throbbing heart her sleeping child,
All she could rescue of the innocent group
That yesterday surrounded her. – Escaped
Almost by miracle!

◎   What do you think this woman might be running from? Where is she
now? What has she left behind?

⦿ The title indicates that she is running from 'the miseries of war'. However, the threats are described so unspecifically that we might imagine many kinds of threat. Do you think this is a valid reading of the text?

Text: Poem (iv)

(iv)   In silent night when rest I took,
       For sorrow near I did not look,
       I waken'd was with thundring nois
       And Piteous shrieks of dreadfull voice.
  5   That fearfull sound of fire and fire,
       Let no man know is my Desire.

       I, starting up, the light did spye,
       And to my God my heart did cry
       To strengthen me in my Distresse
 10   And not to leave me succourlesse.
       Then coming out beheld a space,
       The flame consume my dwelling place.

       And, when I could no longer look,
       I blest his Name that gave and took,
 15   That layd my goods now in the dust:
       Yea so it was, and so 'twas just.
       It was his own: it was not mine;
       Far be it that I should repine.

       He might of All justly bereft,
 20   But yet sufficient for us left.
       When by the Ruines oft I past,
       My sorrowing eyes aside did cast,
       And here and there the places spye
       Where oft I sate, and long did lye.

⦿ What has happened?
⦿ This poem is full of binaries – line 2, and 'fearfull'/'Desire' (lines 5, 6), for example. What others strike you?
⦿ How would you describe 'I''s reaction to the fire?

70

The title of Text: Poem (v) is 'Divergence'. Compare the first line and the last before you read the whole poem to see how they explain the title.

Text: Poem (v)

(v)   When we were friends
and more than friends
my mother love, my sister sun
we went together
5 gloved and girded
to gather the cats turned feral.

You went ahead
for I was then a precious thing
my skin to be protected
10 my blood unspilled
you would have scratched at any heart
had I been hurt.

But the cats cried
to be contained
15 to be uncontained
caught us deep in the flesh.

How we bled,
my broken skin your deepest wound
and by then you wanted me dead.

◎   How do you react to the idea of wild cats in the context of a relationship ending? Does the gender of the participants matter here?

Commentary

In these first five texts, perhaps the most obvious thing they have in common is that something is decidedly wrong. Text (i) addresses a husband ('thee') and the 'things' (line 2) are rivals for the husband's affection, mainly his boring friends. But note how 'I' will try again to recover the situation.

In (ii), the impression is of sexual harassment: 'seducing words'

71

implying she can be corrupted. Words of love have gone too far. Not a new situation!

Text (iii) continues the vein of woman threatened, in a third-person narration (line 3 and the last line perhaps reflecting her own thoughts), as she escapes with one only of her children. The lack of *specific* threat means she could be running from anything.

Text (iv) is one of the earliest of all poems written by a woman in America: her religious (Puritan) beliefs emerge clearly as the tragedy of fire burning down her house is described. The first-person narrative displays emotions from acceptance to anger.

Text (v) brings out the animal in a neat binary between 'precious' and 'deepest wound'. The nature of the relationship is not clear — it could be family, friends or 'more than friends'. Notice also 'when' (line 1) and the movement on to 'then' (line 8) contrasting with 'by then' in the last line.

All of these poems are by women: could any of them have been written by men, do you think? The subjects include husbands, family and home, threats, sexual harassment, and relationships. Is the tone different from poems you have read by men?

Activity

In Text: Poem (vi), the voice is male, but the writer female. Does this confirm what you have already found out, or not?

Text: Poem (vi)

> (**vi**)   A narrow Fellow in the Grass
>   Occasionally rides –
>   You may have met Him – did you not
>   His notice sudden is –
>
>   5   The Grass divides as with a Comb –
>   A spotted shaft is seen –
>   And then it closes at your feet
>   And opens further on –
>
>   He likes a Boggy Acre
> 10   A Floor too cool for Corn –
>   Yet when a Boy, and Barefoot –
>   I more than once at Noon

> Have passed I thought a Whiplash
> Unbraiding in the Sun
> 15 When stooping to secure it
> It wrinkled and was gone -
>
> Several of Nature's People
> I know and they know me -
> I feel for them a transport
> 20 Of cordiality -
>
> But never met this Fellow
> Attended, or alone
> Without a tighter breathing
> And Zero at the Bone -

◎   The images in the second and fourth stanzas are quite different – are they equally valid and effective for you?

◎   What do you imagine the 'narrow Fellow' is?

◎   What impression do the words 'Nature's People' (line 17) give you?

◎   Trace the movement of the text between past and present. What is it about *most*, for you – the fellow, the 'I', nature, man and nature, all (or none) of these? Why?

◎   'Yet when a Boy, and Barefoot' (line 11) clearly identifies the gender of 'I': is it worth talking about a feminine 'sensibility' here?

Commentary

This is quite a different kind of text. Emily Dickinson's punctuation and capital letters make us read it differently from normal, and her regular rhyme and rhythm give a (deceptive) air of simplicity. The snake is a 'Fellow' but moves from friendly to chilling, from the idea of positive Nature ('cordiality') to a threat in the final line. The images are domestic/familiar ('a Comb') and violent ('a Whiplash'); heat and cold too are mixed, past and present, I and you. In short, there is a lot going on here, and the impact is likely to be more complex than with some of the other texts. Gender becomes quite unimportant; though it has to be said that the old image of Emily Dickinson as a sweet little old lady is totally contradicted in this poem. That image must have been a male invention!

Activity

Now refer these thoughts and considerations to another collection of texts (Poems (vii)–(xii)). What makes these poems distinctly women's (if they are!)?

Text: Poem (vii)

(vii)   And the softness of my body will be guarded by embrace
By each button, hook, and lace.
For the man who should loose me is dead,
Fighting with the Duke in Flanders,
In a pattern called a war.
Christ! What are patterns for?

◎   If you take away the last line, does this become a different text? What difference does the last line make, for you?

Text: Poem (viii)

(viii)   I looked for that which is not, nor can be,
And hope deferred made my heart sick in truth:
But years must pass before a hope of youth
        Is resigned utterly.

I watched and waited with a steadfast will:
And though the object seemed to flee away
That I so longed for, ever day by day
        I watched and waited still.

◎   What is this about, in your view?

Text: Poem (ix)

(ix)   Satire should like a polished razor keen,
Wound with a touch that's scarcely felt or seen.
Thine is an oyster's knife, that hacks and hews;
The rage but not the talent to abuse.

◎   What do you get from the tone of this? Would it be different without the second couplet?

◎   She was addressing the poet Alexander Pope – what can you tell about her opinion of his work?

In Text: Poem (x), some words have been taken out in each stanza. How would you complete the lines – and the whole poem?

Text: Poem (x)

(x)   I came to you at _____
With silvery dew on sleeping lotus
Sparkling in my gay hands;
You put my flowers in the sun.

I danced to you at _____
With bright raintree blooms
Flaming in my ardent arms;
You dropped my blossoms in the pond.

I crept to you at _____
With pale lilac orchids
Trembling on my uncertain lips;
You shredded my petals in the sand.

I strode to you at _____
With gravel hard and cold
Clenched in my bitter fists;
You offered me your hybrid orchids,
And I _____.

◎ For you, is 'I' male or female? And 'you'? Does it end positively or negatively for you? (The poet's words were 'sunrise', 'midday', 'sunset', 'midnight' and the final line 'And I crushed them in my despair.')

Text: Poem (xi)

(xi) Wife and servant are the same,
      But only differ in the name;
      For when that fatal knot is tied,
      Which nothing, nothing can divide,
   5 When she the word *Obey* has said,
      And man by law supreme has made,
      Then all that's kind is laid aside,
      And nothing left but state and pride.
      Fierce as an eastern prince he grows,
  10 And all his innate rigour shows:
      Then but to look, to laugh, or speak,
      Will the nuptial contract break.
      Like mutes, she signs alone must make,
      And never any freedom take,
  15 But still be governed by a nod,
      And fear her husband as her god:
      Him still must serve, him still obey,
      And nothing act, and nothing say,
      But what her haughty lord thinks fit,
  20 Who, with the power, has all the wit.
      Then shun, oh! shun that wretched state,
      And all the fawning flatt'rers hate.
      Value yourselves, and men despise:
      You must be proud, if you'll be wise.

◎ Are there any positive notions to counterbalance the generally negative words here?
◎ Would you prefer it to be more balanced?
◎ Does the term 'feminist' apply here? Or to any of the other texts?

The idea of obeying a husband has only recently been questioned, and sometimes eliminated from the marriage vows. Is the central part of text (xi) about the wife being forced into submission – 'nothing act, and nothing say' – still valid? Notice that in line 6 it is the woman who is the subject – *she* makes the man 'supreme'.

The last two lines do seem a bit of a feminist manifesto: it might be worth collecting lines like these from over the years, to see how much they change in their sentiments, attitudes, and ways of speaking.

Text: Poem (xii)

(xii)   Yellow/brown woman
fingers smelling always of onions

My mother raises rare blooms
and waters them with tea
her birth waters sang like rivers
my mother is now me

My mother had a linen dress
the colour of the sky
and stored lace and damask
tablecloths
to pull shame out of her eye.

I am becoming my mother
brown/yellow woman
fingers smelling always of onions.

◎   Again, what can you tell culturally about the text?
◎   What about past/present/future here?

It is interesting how this text emphasises smells and colours, rather than physical characteristics. The idea of deprivation and pride only comes through in the mention of the precious 'lace and damask/ tablecloths', where the 'shame' is compensated for between reader and writer. This poem, 'I Am Becoming My Mother', gave its title to a volume which won the Commonwealth Prize in 1986. The poet, Lorna Goodison, is Jamaican, and lives in New York.

◎   How modern are the themes of texts (vii) to (xii)? And the language?

◎   Pick out two or three of them for comparison.

◎   You might also want to fast forward to a text by Maya Angelou in Unit 8, p. 116.

Activity

We have already seen a range of voices within texts. We are now going to look at how speakers reveal themselves by what they say, and what they don't say.

Text: Poem (xiii) is something of a psycho-drama, where the man speaking (to himself?) reveals a fairly ordinary situation, but with an unexpected twist.

You can either read this text all the way through, to find out what has happened (and why), or take it in stages. You decide.

What can you tell about the speaker, first of all? Male or female?

Text: Poem (xiii)

(xiii)   The rain set early in tonight,
            The sullen wind was soon awake,
            It tore the elm-tops down for spite,
            And did its worst to vex the lake:
    5   I listened with heart fit to break.
            When glided in Porphyria; straight
            She shut the cold out and the storm,
            And kneeled and made the cheerless grate
            Blaze up, and all the cottage warm;
    10   Which done, she rose, and from the form
            Withdrew the dripping cloak and shawl,
            And laid her soiled gloves by, untied
            Her hat and let the damp hair fall,
            And, last, she sat down by my side
    15   And called me. When no voice replied,
            She put my arm about her waist,
            And made her smooth white shoulder bare,
            And all her yellow hair displaced,
            And, stooping, made my cheek lie there,
    20   And spread, o'er all, her yellow hair,

Murmuring how she loved me – she
Too weak, for all her heart's endeavour,
To set its struggling passion free
From pride, and vainer ties dissever,
25 And give herself to me for ever.
But passion sometimes would prevail,
Nor could to-night's gay feast restrain
A sudden thought of one so pale
For love of her, and all in vain:
30 So, she was come through wind and rain.
Be sure I looked up at her eyes
Happy and proud; at last I knew
Porphyria worshipped me; surprise
Made my heart swell, and still it grew
35 While I debated what to do.
That moment she was mine, mine, fair,
Perfectly pure and good: I found
A thing to do, and all her hair
In one long yellow string I wound
40 Three times her little throat around,
And strangled her. No pain felt she;
I am quite sure she felt no pain.
As a shut bud that holds a bee,
I warily oped her lids: again
45 Laughed the blue eyes without a stain.
And I untightened next the tress
About her neck; her cheek once more
Blushed bright beneath my burning kiss:
I propped her head up as before,
50 Only, this time my shoulder bore
Her head, which droops upon it still:
The smiling rosy little head,
So glad it has its utmost will,
That all it scorned at once is fled,
55 And I, its love, am gained instead!
Porphyria's love: she guessed not how
Her darling one wish would be heard.
And thus we sit together now,
And all night long we have not stirred,
60 And yet God has not said a word!

Commentary

Lines 1–5

The first five lines create atmosphere, with a strong negative word in nearly every line – the words are not words we would normally associate with the weather ('sullen', 'vex'), perhaps revealing something about the speaker's own state of mind, 'with heart fit to break' – which is not explained.

Lines 6–15

There is a change in atmosphere signalled in line 6: 'When'. The sentence break might be significant for the change also in him. From line 6 to line 15 Porphyria's actions change the whole mood: you can pick out the contrasts she effects.

The speaker has been remarkably silent so far. Even when she 'called me' (line 15), there is silence. That might suggest something about his character, especially in relation to what we know about his earlier mood.

Lines 15–25

All the actions so far are by Porphyria, and are linked by 'and' – there are more than twenty 'and's in the whole poem. This happens again from line 15 to line 28. This listing of her actions could tell us something about (a) how the speaker sees her, (b) their relationship, and (c) the level of communication between them. He is watching and waiting, observing rather than participating.

- ◎ What contrasts do you notice between action (her) and reflection (him)?
- ◎ When do we begin to hear Porphyria's own voice? How much do we hear her, and how much is it the speaker's thoughts about her? Does he ever actually speak to her? These questions help us build up our impressions of the speaker.
- ◎ Why will she not 'give herself to me for ever' (line 25)? Is this the problem from the beginning?

Lines 26–35

These lines show *his* view of the situation. 'But' (line 26) and 'So' (line 30) tell us about him, his attitudes to her, and to the present situation. Who is 'one so pale' (line 28)? This third-person, more distanced description maintains the sense of an observer we have already noticed.

Why do you think he is surprised (line 33)? Why should he need to debate 'what to do' (line 35)?

Lines 36–41 might surprise you: read on.

Lines 36–48

◎   Was she, or it, 'Perfectly pure and good' (line 37)?
◎   Why does he repeat 'no pain' (lines 41, 42)?
◎   The image in line 43 is quite surprising – is it effective?

Lines 49–60

From line 50, you might detect a note of self-justification. (Maybe the whole text is self-justification.) When he talks of 'its utmost will' (line 53) and 'Her darling one wish' (line 57) – is it him or her? Was he 'Porphyria's love' (line 56) or, as the title puts it, Porphyria's Lover?

The final three lines return to 'And . . . And . . . And . . .' – another list: he has gone back to his role as an observer.

◎   Trace the verb tenses: past, present, present perfect . . .
◎   Most lines are eight-syllable, but some have nine syllables: does this create any effect (lines 22, 24, 25, for instance)?
◎   Do you find this poem chilling, understandable, inexplicable? Are there binaries which help? How much is unsaid, by both participants?

(You might like to check out a recent story by Ruth Rendell called *Lizzie's Lover*, in the volume *Blood Lines* (1995) – an intertextual retelling of the story, which begins and ends with exactly the same words. But the movement within the text is rather different.)

Text: Poem (xiv) is a bit lighter. What can you tell about the speaker?

Text: Poem (xiv)

> (xiv)   As I sat at the café, I said to myself,
> They may talk as they please about what they call pelf,
> They may sneer as they like about eating and drinking,
> But help it I cannot, I cannot help thinking,
>   How pleasant it is to have money, heigh ho!
>   How pleasant it is to have money.

I sit at my table *en grand seigneur*,
And when I have done, throw a crust to the poor;
Not only the pleasure, one's self, of good living,
But also the pleasure of now and then giving.
    So pleasant it is to have money, heigh ho!
    So pleasant it is to have money.

It was but last winter I came up to Town,
But already I'm getting a little renown;
I make new acquaintance where'er I appear,
I am not too shy, and have nothing to fear.
    So pleasant it is to have money, heigh ho!
    So pleasant it is to have money.

I drive through the streets, and I care not a damn;
The people they stare, and they ask who I am;
And if I should chance to run over a cad,
I can pay for the damage, if ever so bad.
    So pleasant it is to have money, heigh ho!
    So pleasant it is to have money.

◎ Do you like him? Does he want you to like him? How do you know he's male anyway? Is he a modern character?

◎ How modern does the text feel? What gives you clues?

◎ Is 'I' likely to be the poet himself, or a character he creates? What point of view is represented – objective, subjective, approving, critical, ironic, or what?

Commentary

This is a good example (the Gavin Ewart text on p. 20–21 is another) of a deliberately ironic technique, creating a voice which the reader can't be expected to like, saying the wrong sort of thing, but revealing fairly common thoughts.

Quite a lot of words and phrases show the language of this text is dated ('pelf' = money, dishonestly obtained; 'I care not a damn'; 'a cad') even though the sentiments might not be.

We have already mentioned Text: Poem (xv) in Unit 2. When does the knight begin to answer the questions?

Text: Poem (xv)

(**xv**)   'O what can ail thee, knight-at-arms,
          Alone and palely loitering?
          The sedge has withered from the lake,
          And no birds sing.

5   'O what can ail thee, knight-at-arms,
          So haggard and so woe-begone?
          The squirrel's granary is full,
          And the harvest's done.

          'I see a lily on thy brow
10 With anguish moist and fever dew;
          And on thy cheek a fading rose
          Fast withereth too.'

          'I met a lady in the meads,
          Full beautiful – a faery's child,
15 Her hair was long, her foot was light,
          And her eyes were wild.

          'I made a garland for her head,
          And bracelets too, and fragrant zone;
          She looked at me as she did love,
20 And made sweet moan.

          'I set her on my pacing steed
          And nothing else saw all day long,
          For sideways would she lean, and sing
          A faery's song.

25 'She found me roots of relish sweet,
          And honey wild and manna dew,
          And sure in language strange she said,
          "I love thee true!"

'She took me to her elfin grot,
30 And there she wept and sighed full sore;
And there I shut her wild, wild eyes
With kisses four.

'And there she lullèd me asleep,
And there I dreamed – Ah! woe betide!
35 The latest dream I ever dreamed
On the cold hill's side.

'I saw pale kings and princes too,
Pale warriors, death-pale were they all;
Who cried – "La Belle Dame sans Merci
40 Hath thee in thrall!"

'I saw their starved lips in the gloam
With horrid warning gapèd wide,
And I awoke and found me here
On the cold hill's side.

45 'And this is why I sojourn here
Alone and palely loitering,
Though the sedge is withered from the lake,
And no birds sing.

◎ In the first two stanzas, what do the third and fourth lines tell us about the season of the year? Is it presented positively or negatively?

◎ What would the traditional expectations of a 'knight' be? What does this knight look like?

◎ So, in his answer, what happened to him? Did he fulfil any of the traditional 'knight' roles in his story? What did she do to him? What went wrong?

◎ How do you interpret the dream? (Death – sex – the past – the future?)

◎ Does he, in fact, answer the basic question?

Commentary

'La Belle Dame sans Merci' (line 39, and the title of the poem) has been translated as 'The Beautiful Woman without Pity'. (A joke version gives it as 'Lovely Lady, No Thanks.') It has, as you would expect, been interpreted in many ways: love and death usually come in somewhere.

But there are a few questions that remain unanswered:

◎   Who is asking the knight the questions (lines 1–2, 5–6)? Is the knight real, alive?
◎   Why 'sedge' (lines 3, 47)? What is sedge anyway? Have the 'birds' (lines 4, 48) gone away?
◎   Where did he take her on his 'steed' (line 21)? Are they now near where she brought him? If so, where did they start from?

Or, are all these questions useless?

We don't know who is questioning the knight, but it is sometimes interpreted as a minstrel, underlining the medieval ballad tone. The knight looks pale and wan, rather than bold and courageous: he is an imaginary figure, but hardly fits the traditional idea of the knight, apart perhaps from the name and the idea of riding off on his steed with the fair damsel. Knights should be active, rather than passive ('loitering'/ 'sojourn'). He should be bold, manly, courageous, conquering his beloved. But the woman's effect on him turns out to be stronger than his on her.

Sedge is a plant which grows densely beside lakes and rivers. It does not seem to be particularly symbolic, but with the absence of birds we might be tempted to think the season is autumn. The journey goes towards failed love, so that the knight emerges as neither a hero, nor a lover – in fact, no true knight at all: neither 'here' (in the 'real' world of now) nor 'there' (in the feminine world). There is a contrast between what the lady offers for his pleasure (roots, honey, manna) and his inability to enjoy them, which leads to his abandonment on the cold hill's side. The power of the knight (and of the kings, princes and warriors) is nothing compared to the sensual power of the woman.

The whole mystery of the poem centres on love and fantasy: the idea of the woman as mysterious and enchanting ties in with the emasculating of the knight, who should typify heroic manhood. So – man as the victim of woman's wiles? Sexual harassment? Male impotence? It could be. *Or* it could be about the impossibility of perfect love, perfect harmony between male/female, nature/culture, active/passive. It depends how 'romantic' you want the text to be. It could be read as a kind of opposite to 'Porphyria's Lover' (pp. 78–79): the two make an interesting contrast.

Extension

The experience of the knight-at-arms ties in with Coleridge's Ancient Mariner, who shot an albatross and was condemned to suffer. Contrast only the first two lines and the last two lines of the whole long poem (Text: Poem (xvi)), to see something of the movement the whole text contains.

Text: Poem (xvi)

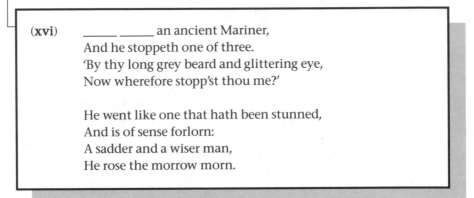

(xvi) _____ _____ an ancient Mariner,
And he stoppeth one of three.
'By thy long grey beard and glittering eye,
Now wherefore stopp'st thou me?'

He went like one that hath been stunned,
And is of sense forlorn:
A sadder and a wiser man,
He rose the morrow morn.

What would you expect the first two words to be?

It is perhaps a little surprising that the words are not 'There was . . .' (or 'Once upon a time there was . . .') but are in the present tense: 'It is . . .'. (This is confirmed by the verb in line 2.)

The 'one of three' is a guest on his way to a wedding. He has to listen to the Mariner's story (part of which we saw in Unit 2). It is the Wedding-Guest who is the subject of the final lines. Are 'sadder' and 'wiser' the same, or a binary? As someone once said, 'Man must suffer to be wise.'

What has happened to the tense of the verb? The text has moved from present (the eternal present of the Mariner's need to tell his story), through the past (the telling of the story, in the past tense), to the past tense – and on towards the future, 'the morrow morn'.

This is a good thing to check out in texts: it expands what we can say about them, and gives them extra time/space resonance. Check back on a few texts you have read, and see how the idea works with them.

Sources

(i) Mehetabel Wright, extract from 'Address to Her Husband' (*c*. 1730); (ii) Sarah Egerton, extract from 'The Repulse to Alcander' (1703); (iii) Charlotte Smith, 'Fragment Descriptive of the Miseries of War' (1797); (iv) Anne Bradstreet, extract from 'Verses Upon the Burning of Our House' (1666); (v) Rebecca Hughes, 'Divergence' (1996); (vi) Emily Dickinson, 'A Narrow Fellow in the Grass' (*c*. 1865); (vii) Amy Lowell, 'Patterns' (1916); (viii) Christina Rossetti, extract from 'A Pause of Thought' (*c*. 1860); (ix) Lady Mary Wortley Montagu, extract from 'To the Imitator of the First Satire of Horace' (*c*. 1734); (x) Hilary Tham, 'Offerings' (1976); (xi) Lady Mary Chudleigh, extract from 'To the Ladies' (1703); (xii) Lorna Goodison, 'I Am Becoming My Mother' (1986); (xiii) Robert Browning, 'Porphyria's Lover' (1836); (xiv) Arthur Hugh Clough, extract from 'How Pleasant It Is to Have Money' from *Dipsychus* (1850/1); (xv) John Keats, 'La Belle Dame sans Merci' (1819/20); (xvi) Samuel Taylor Coleridge, extract from 'The Rime of the Ancient Mariner' (1798).

The images

Activity

Poems are full of images of life, death, and the universe. Some of them work, some don't. How do you react to the ones in Text: Poems (i)–(x)?

Text: Poems (i)-(x)

    (i)   the moon's a balloon

(ii)   All the world's a stage,
        And all the men and women merely players

                (iii)   Love is like a violin

   (iv)   Madam Life's a piece in bloom
           Death goes dogging everywhere;
           She's the tenant of the room,
           He's the ruffian on the stair.

(v)   But treason is not own'd when 'tis descried;
        Successful crimes alone are justified

(vi)   Life is a jest; and all things show it.
        I thought so once; but now I know it.

(vii)   I am a rock.

(viii) My love is like a red, red rose.

(ix)   Man is Heaven's masterpiece.

(x)   So, naturalists observe, a flea
        Hath smaller fleas that on him prey;
        And these have smaller fleas to bite 'em,
        And so proceed *ad infinitum*.
        Thus every poet, in his kind,
        Is bit by him that comes behind.

Commentary

The use of 'is', to affirm a generalisation or a truth for all time, is a stock-in-trade of **representational language**. 'Like' is similarly used in **similes**, and 'as' often in **metaphors**.

You can probably think of, or find, lots of others along the lines of 'Love is . . .'. What makes them interesting is how they work – how they stick in our minds. Which of the ones you have read do you think will turn out to be memorable? Is it because of the words themselves, or something about the image (appropriacy, unexpectedness . . .)?

Activity

Moving on to more elaborate images, how effective do you find the three samples in Text: Poems (xi)–(xiii)?

Text: Poems (xi)–(xiii)

(**xi**)   When the hounds of spring are on winter's traces,
The mother of months in meadow or plain
Fills the shadows and windy places
With lisps of leaves and ripple of rain.

(**xii**)   Stone walls do not a prison make
Nor iron bars a cage;
Minds innocent and quiet take
That for an hermitage;
If I have freedom in my love,
And in my soul am free;
Angels alone, that soar above,
Enjoy such liberty.

(**xiii**)   For lust of knowing what should not be known,
We take the Golden Road to Samarkand.

◎   Text (xi): What month is it about?
◎   Text (xii): Who might the speaker be?
◎   Text (xiii): Is this a real road?

We have seen how often poets make a sweeping generalisation by using
'is' – in Text: Poem (xiv) it's plural. How do you like it?

Text: Poem (xiv)

(**xiv**)   They are not long, the weeping and the laughter,
Love and desire and hate:
I think they have no portion in us after
We pass the gate.

They are not long, the days of wine and roses:
Out of a misty dream
Our path emerges for a while, then closes
Within a dream.

◎   What is the poem about, at first glance?

◎   Is the tone sad or positive (or both)? What is 'the gate' (line 4)?

◎   Do you find it beautiful? How do sounds and the length of the lines contribute to the effect?

Commentary

Text (xi) is about January – the image of the first line perhaps more effective than the 'mother' image, and the alliteration in line 4. Text (xii) contrasts prison/freedom: the speaker may be presumed to be in prison. In text (xiii), Samarkand has come to stand for everything mysterious and oriental.

Text (xiv) is about many things – but transience, the passing nature of all things, is probably the keynote. It could also be about the nature of happiness/sadness, or even life and death. It depends how much you want to read into the images.

The poet Ernest Dowson gave text (xiv) a Latin title – 'Vitae Summa Brevis Spem Nos Vetat Incohare Longam' – which translates as 'the brevity of life stops us from having long-term hopes'. What is your reaction to that? Would you give it a different title?

In the 1890s, the poem was seen as reflecting end-of-century gloom and 'aesthetic' values. Does it still do that? Would you relate it in any way to Matthew Arnold's 'Dover Beach' (in the Poetry Project, pp. 126–127)?

Activity

As readers, we have to decide whether to accept these conceits – if over-done, they become clichés. But often they can surprise us: Simon Armitage, in a very modern poem (Text: Poem (xv)), avoids words like 'like' or 'as', but in his opening words asks us to accept the idea that a matchstick, as it burns, can be a 'sign or symbol'.

Text: Poem (xv)

(xv)   Let this matchstick be a brief biography,
         the sign or symbol
         for the lifetime of a certain someone.

> How a spark of light
> went to his head, but
> how that halo soon came loose,
> became a noose,
> a girdle, then a belt, a Hula-Hoop
> of inflammation spreading through his frame
> to take his legs and black his boots,
>
> and left him spent, bent
> out of line,
> a saint, burnt at the stake,
> the spine.

Does it echo a life? What stages can you trace?

Extension

These are all *ways of seeing*, as William Blake summed them up (in Text: Poem (xvi)):

Text: Poem (xvi)

> (**xvi**)   To see a World in a Grain of Sand,
> And a Heaven in a Wild Flower,
> Hold Infinity in the palm of your hand,
> And Eternity in an hour.

Images like these are all around us. Start a collection from advertisements, newspapers, TV and videos, songs, anywhere you can find them. See if they link with any we have already seen, or if they strike you with new, unexpected impressions.

One of the most frequent ways of conveying an image is by the repetition of a line or lines, to make a chorus or a **refrain**. We are going to look at some famous ones, to see what effect they have.

Activity

Text: Poem (xvii) was one of the best-known poems of its time. But the image of heroism it creates is open to interpretation. As you read, make a note of lines which seem to you heroic and lines which seem *un*heroic.

Text: Poem (xvii)

(xvii)

I

Half a league, half a league,
Half a league onward,
All in the valley of Death
Rode the six hundred.
5   'Forward, the Light Brigade,
Charge for the guns!' he said:
Into the valley of Death
Rode the six hundred.

II

'Forward, the Light Brigade,'
10   Was there a man dismay'd?
Not tho' the soldier knew
Some one had blunder'd:
Theirs not to make reply,
Theirs not to reason why,
15   Theirs but to do and die:
Into the valley of Death
Rode the six hundred.

III

Cannon to right of them,
Cannon to left of them,
20   Cannon in front of them
Volley'd and thunder'd;
Storm'd at with shot and shell,

Boldly they rode and well,
Into the jaws of Death,
25   Into the mouth of Hell
Rode the six hundred.

              IV
Flash'd all their sabres bare,
Flash'd as they turn'd in air
Sabring the gunners there,
30   Charging an army, while
All the world wonder'd:
Plunged in the battery-smoke
Right thro' the line they broke;
Cossack and Russian
35   Reel'd from the sabre-stroke
Shatter'd and sunder'd.
Then they rode back, but not
Not the six hundred.

              V
Cannon to right of them,
40   Cannon to left of them,
Cannon behind them,
Volley'd and thunder'd;
Storm'd at with shot and shell,
While horse and hero fell,
45   They that had fought so well
Came thro' the jaws of Death,
Back from the mouth of Hell,
All that was left of them,
Left of six hundred.

              VI
50   When can their glory fade?
O the wild charge they made!
All the world wonder'd
Honour the charge they made!
Honour the Light Brigade!
55   Noble six hundred!

1   What are the most striking or memorable lines for you? Why are they memorable?

2   How early in the text do we know the charge was a mistake? Who made the mistake?

3   Check through all the repeated lines, and make notes of:

   ◎   how often they are repeated
   ◎   if they are 'heroic' or not
   ◎   if their meaning changes during the poem
   ◎   what other parallelisms you find
   ◎   why you think they are repeated.

4   Who are the enemy?

5   Look at the final verse (no. VI) – would the poem as a whole be different without it? What was 'glorious' about the charge?

6   If 'he' (line 6) is also 'the soldier' (line 11), what does line 12 tell us about him?

7   Lines 13–15 became very famous. It is noticeable that the people who ordered the charge are not mentioned – only the heroes/victims. Is there anything in the poem that suggests or implies *responsibility* for the deaths of the Light Brigade?

8   How many survived?

Commentary

This is the story of a cavalry charge at the Battle of Balaclava (25 October 1854) in the Crimean War (1853–56). It was the first war to be reported in the daily papers, the first war Great Britain had joined since the defeat of Napoleon in 1815, and the first war in modern times that the nation did not win.

When the poem was written, it was read as a patriotic, jingoistic text. Nowadays, it is more tempting to read it as *anti*-war, stressing the blunder and the futility. Marshal some arguments *from the text* for both sides. Can the text actually contain *both* possible interpretations?

It is important to see both sides: to read only the idea we prefer (probably the idea of the tragic waste involved) would be to limit the meaning potential of the text. Tennyson was the national poet in the 1850s, so his role was seen as that of a heroic poet. Whether or not he allowed the ironic possibilities of the text to emerge can never be known. (So we mustn't say 'Tennyson meant ...' – we simply don't know.) Certainly the image that has remained is the image of loss, rather than of heroism. Contrast this with 'Dulce et Decorum Est' (p. 134).

The next refrain (Text: Poem (xviii)) is from the poem Oscar Wilde wrote after his release from prison. What images do you get of prison and of despair?

Text: Poem (xviii)

(**xviii**)   I walked, with other souls in pain,
        Within another ring,
        And was wondering if the man had done
        A great or little thing,
5   When a voice behind me whispered low,
        'That fellow's got to swing.'

        Dear Christ! The very prison walls
        Suddenly seemed to reel,
        And the sky above my head became
10   Like a casque of scorching steel;
        And, though I was a soul in pain,
        My pain I could not feel.

        I only knew what hunted thought
        Quickened his step, and why
15   He looked upon the garish day
        With such a wistful eye;
        The man had killed the thing he loved,
        And so he had to die.

        Yet each man kills the thing he loves,
20   By each let this be heard,
        Some do it with a bitter look,
        Some with a flattering word,
        The coward does it with a kiss,
        The brave man with a sword!

25   Some kill their love when they are young,
        And some when they are old;
        Some strangle with the hands of Lust,
        Some with the hands of Gold:

> The kindest use a knife, because
> 30   The dead so soon grow cold.
>
> Some love too little, some too long,
> Some sell, and others buy;
> Some do the deed with many tears,
> And some without a sigh:
> 35   For each man kills the thing he loves,
> Yet each man does not die.

◎   Where do you think they are in the first verse? When does it become clear?

◎   Whose is 'his' (line 14)?

◎   How does 'Yet' (line 19) change the movement of the poem?

◎   The last three verses are more general, about 'each man'; the first three about one man, and 'I''s reactions. What other binaries can you find?

Commentary

Do you agree that 'each man kills the thing he loves' (lines 19, 35)? How do you react to the list of ways to kill? Would you add more?

Do you prefer to see this poem as personal (the poet regretting his mistakes), or as a plea against hanging? How much does the text give you objectively, and how much is your own subjective reaction?

The idea of 'each man kills the thing he loves' has been taken to refer to Oscar Wilde's own martyrdom (he could have got out of the country and escaped jail, but didn't; so killed his own successful career). But, as a wider image of human fallibility, the text's resonances become endless. It was sung by Jeanne Moreau in the Fassbinder movie *Querelle*.

Activity

In Text: Poem (xix), the sentiment and the imagery are obvious. What can you tell *from the language* (and the exclamation marks!) about when it might have been written?

Text: Poem (xix)

(xix)   The trumpet of Liberty sounds through the world,
         And the universe starts at the sound;
         Her standard Philosophy's hand has unfurled,
         And the nations are thronging around.

Chorus: Fall, tyrants, fall! fall! fall!
             These are the days of liberty!
             Fall, tyrants, fall!

How noble the ardour that seizes the soul!
How it bursts from the yoke and the chain!
What power can the fervour of Freedom control,
Or its terrible vengeance restrain?

         Fall, tyrants, fall! [. . .]

Proud castles of despotism, dungeons and cells,
The tempest shall sweep you away;
From the east to the west the dread hurricane swells,
And the tyrants are chilled with dismay.

         Fall, tyrants, fall! [. . ..]

Shall Britons the chorus of liberty hear
With a cold and insensible mind?
No, - the triumphs of freedom each Briton shall share,
And contend for the rights of mankind.

         Fall, tyrants, fall!

◉   Check the adjectives used, positively and negatively. What do they
     contribute to the tone?
◉   What kind of images are used?

Commentary

Do you find the text realistic, idealistic, or what? What about the
emphasis on 'Britons' in the last verse? Where do you think this 'Liberty'
is happening? (The poem's title is 'The Trumpet of Liberty'.)
    Would it be possible to write something like that nowadays? Give
reasons.

99

William Wordsworth (Text: Poem (xx)) wrote at about the same time (about the French Revolution of 1789):

Text: Poem (xx)

> (**xx**)   Bliss was it in that dawn to be alive,
> But to be young was very heaven!

Do you think such enthusiasm is *always* bound to lead to disappointment and disillusion, as it did in the 1790s? Is it, however, necessary to have such ideals and enthusiasms? Or are they not appropriate to the modern world?

We tend to distrust this kind of exclamatory writing nowadays — even describing it negatively as romantic.

Finally, one of the most resonant of all refrains, 'Timor mortis conturbat me' (Text: Poem (xxi)). It is Latin for 'the fear of death troubles me'. As you read, how does the poet make a binary from it?

Text: Poem (xxi)

> (**xxi**)   Our plesance here is all vane glory,
> This fals warld is bot transitory,
> The flesche is brukle, the Fend is sle:
>   *Timor mortis conturbat me.*
>
> 5   The stait of man dois change and vary,
> Now wound, now seik, now blith, now sary,
> Now dansand mery, now like to dee:
>   *Timor mortis conturbat me.*

> No stait in erd heir standis sickir;
> 10   As with the wynd wavis the wickir
> Wavis this warldis vanite:
>   *Timor mortis conturbat me.* [...]
>
>
> He sparis no lord for his piscence,
> Na clerk for his intelligence,
> 15   His awful strak may no man fle:
>   *Timor mortis conturbat me.*

'brukle' (line 3) = weak, brittle; 'sle' (line 3) = sly; 'seik' (line 6) = sick; 'sary' (line 6) = sorry; 'dansand' (line 7) = dancing; 'No stait in erd heir standis sickir' (line 9) = No state here on earth stands secure; 'wickir' (line 10) = straw; 'piscence' (line 13) = power, puissance; 'strak' (line 15) = stroke.

◎   How much is this about change, and how much about death?

◎   Apart from the refrain, can you find other devices the poet uses?

◎   Who is 'He' (line 13)?

Life is constantly related to the chorus of death: all levels of society are invoked, and, like the Dowson text, transitoriness becomes the only certainty.

Again, does this reflect an old worry, or a modern concern too?

From the language, it is clear that this text is older than 'The Trumpet of Liberty'. The old words and spellings in particular do not have the forms that modern English, even in the 1790s, displayed.

Extension

Try out a dating exercise on some poems – see what you can tell just by looking at the language or the form or the subject matter and try to put a date or a period to them. You can then check the list of texts on p. 143 to see how close you were.

As you become more familiar with different kinds of poetic language there will be more and more tell-tale signs that you will recognise.

Sources

(i) e.e. cummings, extract from 'N&: VII' (1925); (ii) William Shakespeare, extract from '*As You Like It*' (1599/1600); (iii) Song title, 1960; (iv) W.E. Henley, extract from 'To W.R.' from *Echoes* (1888); (v) John Dryden, extract from 'The Medal' (1682); (vi) John Gay, 'My Own Epitaph' (1720); (vii) Song title, 1966; (viii) Robert Burns, extract from 'My Love Is Like a Red, Red Rose' (*c.* 1796); (ix) Francis Quarles, extract from 'Emblems' (1643); (x) Jonathan Swift, extract from 'On Poetry' (1733); (xi) Algernon Swinburne, extract from 'Atalanta in Calydon' (1865); (xii) Richard Lovelace, extract from 'To Althea from Prison' (1642); (xiii) James Elroy Flecker, extract from 'Hassan' (1922); (xiv) Ernest Dowson, 'Vitae Summa Brevis Spem Nos Vetat Incohare Longam' (1896); (xv) Simon Armitage, 'Let This Matchstick Be a Brief Biography' (1995); (xvi) William Blake, 'Auguries of Innocence' (*c.* 1803); (xvii) Alfred, Lord Tennyson, 'The Charge of the Light Brigade' (1854); (xviii) Oscar Wilde, extract from *The Ballad of Reading Gaol* (1898); (xix) John Taylor, 'The Trumpet of Liberty' (1791); (xx) William Wordsworth, extract from 'The French Revolution As It Appeared to Enthusiasts' (1809) and *The Prelude*; (xxi) William Dunbar, extract from 'Lament for the Makers' (*c.* 1507).

That was then, this is now

One of the most enjoyable discoveries in poetry is how the same ideas come back again and again - but always in slightly different ways. Being out of work, or living on very low wages, doesn't change much.

Activity

What do the two poems in Text: Poems (i)-(ii) have in common?

Text: Poems (i)-(ii)

(i)

He who knows sorrow,   despoiled of joys,
Sits heavy of mood;   to his heart it seemeth
His measure of misery   meeteth no end.
Yet well may he think   how oft in this world
5   The wise Lord varies   His ways to men,
Granting wealth and honor   to many an eorl,
To others awarding   a burden of woe.

And so I can sing   of my own sad plight
Who long stood high   as the Heodenings' bard,
10 Deor my name   dear to my lord
Mild was my service   for many a winter,
Kindly my king   till Heorrenda came
Skillful in song   and usurping the land-right
Which once my gracious lord   granted to me.

15 That evil ended.   So also may this!

(ii)

I was the love that chose my mother out;
I joined two lives and from the union burst;
My weakness and my strength without a doubt
Are mine alone for ever from the first:
5 It's just the very same with a difference in the name
As 'Thy will be done.' You say if it durst!

They say it daily up and down the land
As easy as you take a drink, it's true;
But the difficultest go to understand,
10 And the difficultest job a man can do,
Is to come it brave and meek with thirty bob a week,
And feel that that's the proper thing to do.

It's a naked child against a hungry wolf;
It's playing bowls upon a splitting wreck;
15 It's walking on a string across a gulf
With millstones fore-and-aft about your neck;
But the thing is daily done by many and many a one;
And we fall, face forward, fighting, on the deck.

They are thematically similar, but they achieve their effects differently.
What differences can you pick out? How modern would you say they are?
What about the imagery?

Commentary

There is, in these two texts, both acceptance of your fate and complaint against it.

Deor was replaced as 'the Heodenings' bard' (line 9) by the charmingly named Heorrenda, and lost his 'land-right' (line 13). Yet the poem is a *consolatio*: what makes it positive, if it is?

◎ How does the first stanza of 'Deor's Lament' lead to, or link with, the second?

◎ In the second poem, what is the basic difficulty? What do 'It's' (line 5) and 'It's' (lines 13, 14, 15) refer to? And what do you think 'come it' (line 11) means?

Deor speaks of sorrow in general; then, after 'so' (line 8) of his own particular plight – secure in his place 'till Heorrenda came' (line 12). The final line can be read totally positively, or with some irony – 'may' not 'will'!

In (ii), the image of 'a naked child against a hungry wolf' (line 13) is close to 'keeping the wolf from the door' – the standard image of earning a living, going back a long way in origin. The single word 'It's' is the whole struggle encapsulated in the images which follow. The whole poem moves from birth, in the first two lines, to death (again in an image) in the final line; it is much more negative than the ending of 'Deor's Lament'.

The first of these texts is over a thousand years old. The split line anticipates the later ten-syllable lines we have found so often, with a characteristic **caesura** in the middle, giving a kind of spoken rhythm.

'Thirty Bob a Week' (ii) dates from 1894, and represents £1.50 in old money, long before there was any talk of a minimum wage. Is there any *consolatio* here?

◎ What can you tell about the speaker's birth?

◎ Line 6 contains a Biblical reference: what kind of tone do you find in the second half of this line? It might be interpreted as 'You [the reader] say if God's will dare [be done].' Do you accept that reading?

◎ Why should a man 'come it brave and meek' (line 11)? Does 'I' think it is 'the proper thing for you' (line 12)?

What can you tell about social classes from these two texts? What binaries do you find? Do you think the rhymes help 'Thirty Bob a Week'? Would 'Deor's Lament' benefit from rhymes? (You could try rewriting it in rhyme.)

The next two (Text: Poems (iii)–(iv)) look at the heart; metaphorically (of course) poets tend to treat it as the seat of the emotions. How do you find these two approaches?

Text: Poems (iii)–(iv)

(iii)   I took my heart in my hand
      (O my love, O my love),
      I said: Let me fall or stand,
      Let me live or die,
5   But this once hear me speak –
      (O my love, O my love) –
      Yet a woman's words are weak;
      You should speak, not I.

      You took my heart in your hand
10 With a friendly smile,
      With a critical eye you scanned,
      Then set it down,
      And said: It is still unripe,
      Better wait awhile;
15 Wait while the skylarks pipe,
      Till the corn grows brown.

      As you set it down it broke –
      Broke, but I did not wince;
      I smiled at the speech you spoke,
20 At your judgement that I heard:
      But I have not often smiled
      Since then, nor questioned since,
      Nor cared for corn-flowers wild,
      Nor sung with the singing bird.

(iv)   I saw a creature, naked, bestial,
      Who, squatting upon the ground,
      Held his heart in his hands,
      And ate of it.
      I said, 'Is it good, friend?'
      'It is bitter – bitter,' he answered;
      'But I like it
      Because it is bitter,
      And because it is my heart.'

◎ How would you describe the tone of each 'I'? What do the adjectives tell you about 'I' and about 'you' in the first poem? What change is there at line 21?

◎ How do you interpret the 'creature' in the second poem? Is it real?

◎ Which of the two do you like better?

Extension

'Deor's Lament' and 'Thirty Bob a Week' are both longer than the extracts you have read. You might like to find the complete texts and see how they relate to the extracts.

Activity

Another way of contrasting poems is *synchronically* – that is, to put together texts that were written at more or less the same time. For example, Walt Whitman and Emily Dickinson, although contemporaries, could hardly be more different in what and how they wrote.

◎ What differences do you notice immediately in the three poems in Text: Poems (v)–(vii)?

Text: Poems (v)–(vii)

(v)   Bearing the bandages, water and sponge,
Straight and swift to my wounded I go,
Where they lie on the ground after the battle brought in,
Where their priceless blood reddens the grass the ground,
5 Or to the rows of the hospital tent, or under the roof'd hospital,
To the long rows of cots up and down each side I return,
To each and all one after another I draw near, not one do I miss,
An attendant follows holding a tray, he carries a refuse pail,
Soon to be fill'd with clotted rags and blood, emptied, and fill'd again.

10 I onward go, I stop,
With hinged knees and steady hand to dress wounds,
I am firm with each, the pangs are sharp yet unavoidable,
One turns to me his appealing eyes - poor boy! I never knew you,
Yet I think I could not refuse this moment to die for you, if that would save you.

> (vi)   Much Madness is divinest Sense -
> To a discerning Eye -
> Much Sense - the starkest Madness -
> 'Tis the Majority
> In this, as All, prevail -
> Assent - and you are sane -
> Demur - you're straightway dangerous -
> And handled with a Chain -
>
> (vii)   I sing to use the Waiting
> My Bonnet but to tie
> And shut the Door unto my House
> No more to do have I
>
> Till His best step approaching
> We journey to the Day
> And tell each other how We sung
> To Keep the Dark away.

- What is 'I' doing in text (v) (by Whitman)? What does line 2 tell you about his commitment? And lines 12 to 14?
- In the Dickinson texts, the line lengths and punctuation are quite different. How do they help the overall effect of the poems? How significant are the adjectives in 'Much Madness ...'? What is it about, in your own words? Are there binaries here?
- 'I sing ...' – Whitman also used the verb 'to sing' in his poetry. Why do you think they liked the word? (You might also like to check out 'I, Too' – later in this unit.)
- In 'I Sing to Use the Waiting', how do you relate the first line to the next three? Whose is 'His best step' (line 5), do you think? Compare the first line and the last – how do they link? What is this poem about – singing, waiting ...?

Commentary

The main differences between Walt Whitman and Emily Dickinson are in line length, punctuation, and the rhythm that results. Whitman's lines flow, moving the action along in a narrative, where Dickinson stops on a thought, a moment. The second Dickinson text contrasts with the first: it is less hesitant and conversational, and unusual in being all one continuous sentence, maybe representing one continuous thought.

Whitman actually worked as a wound-dresser in the American Civil War of the 1860s – the text is autobiographical.

Activity

From more or less the same period, John Clare and John Keats show how different the so-called Romantics can be: one describing solitude and 'ship-wreck', the other writing one of the great celebrations of the seasons (Text: Poems (viii)–(ix)). At a first reading, which do you identify with more?

Text: Poems (viii)-(ix)

(viii)   I am: yet what I am none cares or knows,
My friends forsake me like a memory lost;
I am the self-consumer of my woes,
They rise and vanish in oblivious host,
Like shades in love and death's oblivion lost;
And yet I am, and live with shadows tost

Into the nothingness of scorn and noise,
Into the living sea of waking dreams,
Where there is neither sense of life nor joys,
But the vast shipwreck of my life's esteems;
And e'en the dearest - that I loved the best -
Are strange - nay, rather stranger than the rest.

I long for scenes where man has never trod,
A place where woman never smiled or wept;
There to abide with my Creator, God,
And sleep as I in childhood sweetly slept:
Untroubling and untroubled where I lie,
The grass below - above the vaulted sky.

(ix)   Season of mists and mellow fruitfulness!
Close bosom-friend of the maturing sun:
Conspiring with him how to load and bless
With fruit the vines that round the thatch-eaves run;
5 To bend with apples the mossed cottage-trees,
And fill all fruit with ripeness to the core;
To swell the gourd, and plump the hazel shells
With a sweet kernel; to set budding more,
And still more, later flowers for the bees,
10 Until they think warm days will never cease,
For Summer has o'erbrimmed their clammy cells.

Who hath not seen thee oft amid thy store?
Sometimes whoever seeks abroad may find
Thee sitting careless on a granary floor,
15 Thy hair soft-lifted by the winnowing wind,
Or on a half-reaped furrow sound asleep,
Drowsed with the fume of poppies, while thy hook
Spares the next swath and all its twinèd flowers;
And sometimes like a gleaner thou dost keep
20 Steady thy laden head across a brook;
Or by a cider press, with patient look,
Thou watchest the last oozings hours by hours.

Where are the songs of Spring? Ay, where are they?
Think not of them, thou hast thy music too, –
25 While barrèd clouds bloom the soft-dying day,
And touch the stubble-plains with rosy hue;
Then in a wailful choir the small gnats mourn
Among the river sallows, borne aloft
Or sinking as the light wind lives or dies;
30 And full-grown lambs loud bleat from hilly bourn;
Hedge-crickets sing; and now with treble soft
The redbreast whistles from a garden-croft;
And gathering swallows twitter in the skies.

Clare ('I am . . .')

◎ There are a lot of contrasts here: I/my friends, present/past, etc. Pick out as many as you can, and say which seem to you the most significant.

◎ How do the rhyme scheme and verse structure help convey 'I''s feelings?

◎ Does the poem give you more a sense of loss, of longing, or of affirmation of identity?

◎ Does it move towards a future, or remain in the present?

Keats ('Season of mists . . .')

◎ What is the poet addressing? Who is 'thee' (line 12)?

◎ In the third verse, is there an answer to the opening question? What binaries do you find between, for example, growing and dying?

◎ Pick out words and phrases which contain contrasts, such as 'bloom the soft-dying day' (line 25) or 'borne aloft / Or sinking' (lines 28–9). How do they convey the ideas between the binaries of positive and negative, growing and dying, etc.?

◎ Words like 'maturing' (line 2) and 'ripeness' (line 6) dominate: pick out a few of these, then see if you can find *negative* words.

◎ Who are 'they' (line 10)?

◎ Look at the adjectives – how many of them appeal to the senses (touch, sight, smell, taste, hearing)? Which words and phrases do you find particularly effective?

◎ Who is 'sitting' (line 14)? Who is 'sound asleep' (line 16)?

◎ Which words and phrases give an idea of time?

◎ Autumn is a time of falling leaves, of losing warmth, of ending: how does Keats handle these concepts in this ode, 'To Autumn'?

◎ The third stanza contains many sounds: are they all positive?

◎ What are 'full-grown lambs' (line 30)? What have they to do with 'Spring' (line 23)? Or with autumn, for that matter?

◎ '. . . and now' (line 31) signals a shift in time. In what season do robins ('The redbreast', line 32) usually appear? And 'swallows' (line 33)?

◎ The final lines could be read as a rapid conflation of autumn, through winter, to spring. Or do you prefer to see the poem as just about autumn? Is the main idea for you, maturity, death, growth, renewal, richness, harvest, or something else?

◎ How would you tie this in with Shelley's famous last line to his 'Ode to the West Wind' (1819/20):

> If Winter comes, can Spring be far behind?

◎   How literally should the line be taken?

Commentary

'I am . . .' focuses on the speaker: all others, even those closest to him, have abandoned him. But the pervading sense of solitude by the end is tempered by the idea of harmony with God and nature. There is no sense of existential loneliness at the end: the darkest moment of 'nothingness' is between lines 6 and 10 – echoes of Keats's 'When I Have Fears' on p. 26?

The questions about Keats's ode 'To Autumn' should bring out the positive insistence on growth and maturity throughout the text. There is no mention of falling leaves, or any of the traditional 'fall' ideas of autumn. It is all growth, harvest, produce, *extra*. The **personification** of autumn – 'thee' (line 12), 'Thee' (line 14), 'Thou' (line 22) – is as a conspirator with the sun (line 3), a sleepy harvester (line 16), and 'a gleaner' (line 19), confirming the positive productive tone.

The question at line 23 moves on to dismiss Spring and celebrate the sounds of Autumn. 'Full-grown lambs' move Spring forward to Autumn (and sheep!), and a slight life/death binary begins to come in, in lines 25–29 ('soft-dying day', 'wailful choir', 'mourn', 'lives or dies'). But as soon as that note is mentioned, it is transcended: the sounds move rapidly from autumn, in line 30, to the winter song of the robin ('redbreast', line 32) and on to the following spring.

It is worth asking how much of these two poems is in the present tense – but both look towards a future.

So what is poetry today, compared to what it used to be?

Free verse, without rhyme and the regular rhythm of **scansion**, is more frequently used than it was – but rhyme is by no means dead.

Activity

Text: Poem (x), though written long before, is probably the best-known poem of the 1990s, because of its use in a movie. Look at the form, the rhyme, and the movement from inside to . . . where?

Text: Poem (x)

(x)   Stop all the clocks, cut off the telephone,
Prevent the dog from barking with a juicy bone,
Silence the pianos and with muffled drum
Bring out the coffin, let the mourners come.

5   Let aeroplanes circle moaning overhead
Scribbling on the sky the message He Is Dead,
Put crêpe bows round the white necks of the public doves,
Let the traffic policemen wear black cotton gloves.

He was my North, my South, my East and West,
10 My working week and my Sunday rest,
My noon, my midnight, my talk, my song;
I thought that love would last for ever: I was wrong.

The stars are not wanted now: put out every one;
Pack up the moon and dismantle the sun;
15 Pour away the ocean and sweep up the wood.
For nothing now can ever come to any good.

- Three stanzas begin with imperatives: how possible are they, verse by verse?
- Trace the movement, and parallel it with the possibility/impossibility of the requests.
- Which line do you find most moving? Why?
- Is 'I' female?
- How is the third stanza different?
- How much is the poem personal, and how much universal? When do you think it becomes more universal?
- Do you detect any hints at religion, or references to it?
- How do you interpret 'the wood' (line 15) – the forest and trees, the wood at the bottom of the seas, or what?
- Hamlet says at one point in Shakespeare's play, 'It is not nor it cannot come to good.' Could the last line be an echo of that? Or do you not like that kind of cross-reference?
- Does the text move between past, present, and future, as you see it?

In the movie, the poem was read by a man at his gay lover's funeral. Would you have expected 'I' to be female? Does the fact that the poet himself, W.H. Auden, was gay make any difference?

113

Commentary

The poem moves from domestic, indoors, outside to the open air, where the requests become less easily do-able, until they reach a cosmic level of impossibility in the final stanza. Line 9 takes the 'geography' of the text out from city to globe, but lines 11 and 12 make the most personal, individual impact of the whole poem – the only lines in which 'I' appears. After this, the verb in line 13 goes into the passive voice.

Activity

The Auden text is one example of how a poem can be reread in different ways. Straight/gay is a much more readily accepted binary that it was when A.E. Housman wrote Text: Poem (xi), although it is now very clear what the poem is about. Could it be read either way?

Text: Poem (xi)

(xi)   Because I liked you better
        Than suits a man to say,
        It irked you, and I promised
        To throw the thought away.

  5   To put the world between us
        We parted, stiff and dry;
        'Good-bye,' said you, 'forget me.'
        'I will, no fear,' said I.

        If here, where clover whitens
 10   The dead man's knoll, you pass,
        And no tall flower to meet you
        Starts in the trefoiled grass,

        Halt by the headstone naming
        The heart no longer stirred,
 15   And say the lad that loved you
        Was one that kept his word.

◎   What overall impression does this give you? What does the phrase 'suits a man to say' (line 2) suggest to you? Why should the loved one be 'irked' (line 3)?

◎   What has happened in the third stanza? Who is 'you' (line 15)? Who is 'the lad' (line 15)?

◎   How much is it a love poem?

Activity

Is the loss in Text: Poem (xii) similar?

AIDS has given rise to a lot of writing. This poem was written in 1984, very early in the epidemic. What is its impact on you?

Text: Poem (xii)

(xii)   Isaac and Elijah
         Were a beautiful couple.
         Lived in Jackson, Mississippi.
         We met them: Went to see
         Dressed to Kill

         Loved it

         Went home, Ate
         Creole,
         Made love.

         Kept in touch
         Three years.

         This June Elijah died of AIDS.
         This is not a poem about Elijah dying of AIDS.
         I love the memory of him.

         But God I weep for Isaac.

◎   What can you tell about Isaac and Elijah? And about 'We' (line 4)?

◎   How do the punctuation and the line lengths affect the way you read?

115

◎ Do you think this is more about love, AIDS, death, memory, or what?
◎ How do past, present, and future relate here? Would it be different if it were written today? How much do you think modern poetry can, or should, address such issues as AIDS, or women's rights, or social deprivation?
◎ How many of the texts so far have had any kind of social commitment?

Commentary

These last three poems show different aspects of male gay writing: in the first, the absence of gender-specific pronouns allows for open reading (which may or may not be considered preferable); the second shows the restrained 'stiff-upper-lip' attitude, where reticence and the unstated underscore both the strength and the waste of love. The third is more obviously explicit, but the theme has gone beyond the limits of sexual orientation.

The subject of all three poems is love and loss, but quite different techniques have been used to express it. The Auden stanzas (x) use more syllables than the Housman (xi), and text (xii) uses free verse. Whether the impact of each one is different could be discussed.

Activity

As you read Text: Poem (xiii), decide whom 'too' refers to. Why has 'I' been excluded up till now?

Text: Poem (xiii)

(xiii)   I, too, sing America.

I am the darker brother.
They send me to eat in the kitchen
When company comes,
5 But I laugh,
An' eat well,
And grow strong.

Tomorrow,
I'll sit at the table
10 When company comes.
Nobody'll dare
Say to me,
'Eat in the kitchen,'
Then.

15 Besides,
They'll see how beautiful I am
And be ashamed.

I, too, am America.

Activity

◎ Why does 'I' say things will be different in the future? Why should 'They' (lines 3, 16) 'be ashamed' (line 17)?

◎ This poem was published in 1925. Have things changed?

◎ Do you find this powerful, simplistic, out of date, valid, or what?

Commentary

This is one of the best-known texts by a black poet in the early twentieth century. Like the text before it, it uses free verse; here a powerful first-person voice combines presence with what can almost be seen as a threat. For outsiders, it may seem necessary to make this kind of statement – but exclusion goes on, the world over. (Cross-refer to Valerie Bloom, p. 54, for instance.)

Activity

The perception of women's roles has not necessarily changed – remember the texts in Unit 6. Is Text: Poem (xiv) complaining?

117

Text: Poem (xiv)

(xiv)   I've got the children to tend
       The clothes to mend
       The floor to mop
       The food to shop
5   Then the chicken to fry
       The baby to dry
       I got company to feed
       The garden to weed
       I've got the shirts to press
10 The tots to dress
       The cane to be cut
       I gotta clean up this hut
       Then see about the sick
       And the cotton to pick.

15 Shine on me, sunshine
       Rain on me, rain
       Fall softly, dewdrops
       And cool my brow again.

       Storm, blow me from here
20 With your fiercest wind
       Let me float across the sky
       'Til I can rest again.

       Fall gently, snowflakes
       Cover me with white
25 Cold icy kisses and
       Let me rest tonight.

       Sun, rain, curving sky
       Mountain, oceans, leaf and stone
       Star shine, moon glow
30 You're all that I can call my own.

◎   How is the first part different from the second?
◎   Overall, is it positive or negative in tone?
◎   Where do you think this woman is?
◎   Is it a celebration, or what?
◎   The title is 'Woman Work'. Is this a good title, in your opinion?

Again a first-person speaker, but the way she speaks is different from the assertiveness of the Langston Hughes text (xiii). Until line 14 it is a list, rhyming; but then it moves into a different mode, using gentle imperatives to the elements and the sky. (Compare the imperatives in 'Stop All the Clocks', text (x).) These imperatives help the speaker transcend her daily round: contrast the gentleness of the final four stanzas with the harsher rhythm and rhymes of the first part ('cut'/'hut', 'sick'/'pick').

But a woman poet need not concern herself only with women's roles. What is Text: Poem (xv) about?

Text: Poem (xv)

(xv)   Nobody heard him, the dead man,
        But still he lay moaning:
        I was much further out than you thought
        And not waving but drowning.

5   Poor chap, he always loved larking
        And now he's dead
        It must have been too cold for him his heart gave way,
        They said.

        Oh, no no no, it was too cold always
10   (Still the dead one lay moaning)
        I was much too far out all my life
        And not waving but drowning.

◎   What happened, before the first verse? Where is 'he' now?
◎   Who says each of these lines: 3–4; 5–7; 9; 11–12?

The title, 'Not Waving but Drowning', has become almost a catchphrase. Is it a universal metaphor? Can you identify with it?

This has become one of the most famous images of modern isolation; a simple expression of the difficulty of keeping up. The voices are the drowning man's (lines 3–4), an observer (possibly the poet) (lines 5–7), and the drowning man again (lines 9, 11–12).

Notice how the pronoun helps the first line: it would be weaker as 'Nobody heard the dead man.'

Activity

Seamus Heaney is the most recent Irish poet to have won the Nobel Prize for Literature. In Text: Poem (xvi) he famously uses the metaphor of digging, to explore both his own past and the history of Ireland itself.

Text: Poem (xvi)

(xvi)   Between my finger and my thumb
The squat pen rests; snug as a gun.

Under my window, a clean rasping sound
When the spade sinks into gravelly ground:
5 My father, digging. I look down

Till his straining rump among the flowerbeds
Bends low, comes up twenty years away
Stooping in rhythm through potato drills
Where he was digging.

10 The coarse boot nestled on the lug, the shaft
Against the inside knee was levered firmly.
He rooted out tall tops, buried the bright edge deep
To scatter new potatoes that we picked
Loving their cool hardness in our hands.

15 By God, the old man could handle a spade.
Just like his old man.

My grandfather cut more turf in a day
Than any other man on Toner's bog.
Once I carried him milk in a bottle

20   Corked sloppily with paper. He straightened up
      To drink it, then fell to right away

      Nicking and slicing neatly, heaving sods
      Over his shoulder, going down and down
      For the good turf. Digging.

25   The cold smell of potato mould, the squelch and slap
      Of soggy peat, the curt cuts of an edge
      Through living roots awaken in my head.
      But I've no spade to follow men like them.

      Between my finger and my thumb
30   The squat pen rests.
      I'll dig with it.

◉   Where is 'I' in the first five lines? Does he hear or see the digging?

◉   Which word in line 6 moves the poem in time? How far back? When does it come back to the present?

◉   Pick out words which create sounds of digging, and others which show actions and movements.

◉   Apart from sight and sound, are there any other senses involved (touch, taste, smell)?

◉   What makes this poem particularly Irish, for you? How do present, past, and future relate here?

◉   Heaney makes many telling details very precise: pick out one or two that you find particularly vivid. How much do adjectives and adverbs contribute to this?

◉   There are also quite a few very specific vocabulary items to do with digging. Pick out some of them, and see what they add to the overall effect.

◉   How do you like the first stanza/final stanza contrast? What does it tell you about the poet's role?

Commentary

Potatoes have considerable resonance in the Irish context, because of the famines of the mid-nineteenth century. Heaney's achievement is to bring together the agricultural past, the sense of family and continuity, and the presence of violence in today's Ireland.

The movement of time, in line 7, is a visual link between present (seeing and hearing) and memory of personal involvement with the past. Touch and smell, along with memory, unite in lines 25–27, bringing together all the senses apart from taste (but drinking the milk – lines 20–21 – could be said to bring that sense in too).

The repetition of the opening lines suddenly opens up a whole new future, and brings together agricultural and written culture in a spectacular new way.

Extension

What becomes famous depends on many things. What stays famous is different: it has to appeal over years, in different places and circumstances, and probably for lots of different reasons.

We are now going to look at 'one-liners' – very short quotations – that have lasted, to see what their appeal might be, then follow them in the Poetry Project with some of the poems that are fairly generally reckoned to be among the classics. Is it easier to say why a line (or two) should last, or easier to say of a whole poem, 'Yes, that works'?

Pick out your favourites from the dozen in Text: Poems (xvii)–(xxviii), and say why they work for you. Do they contain movement, even in a single line?

Text: Poems (xvii)-(xxviii)

(xvii)   I think continually of those who were truly great.

(xviii)   The still sad music of humanity.

(xix)   Ah, but a man's reach should exceed his grasp,
Or what's a heaven for?

(xx)   Do not go gentle into that good night,
Old age should burn and rave at close of day;
Rage, rage against the dying of the light.

(xxi)   Laugh and the world laughs with you
Weep, and you weep alone.

(xxii)   Give me your tired, your poor,
Your huddled masses yearning to breathe free.

(**xxiii**)   A child said *What is the grass?* fetching it to one with full hands
How could I answer the child? I do not know what it is any more than he.

   (**xxiv**)   Soothed with the sound, the king grew vain,
Fought all his battles o'er again.

   (**xxv**)   They flee from me, that sometime did me seek.

      (**xxvi**)   When Israel was in Egypt land,
Let my people go,
Oppressed so hard they could not stand,
Let my people go.

Go down, Moses,
(**xxvii**)   Better to reign in hell, than serve in heav'n.   Way-down in Egypt land,
Tell old Pharaoh
   (**xxviii**)   This is the way the world ends   To let my people go.
Not with a bang but a whimper.

◎   Did you find some of these twelve snippets banal? Does that stop them being true? Compare them with the other short quotations throughout the book.

◎   Are there lines you would like to add to the list? Collect a few, from songs, poems, anywhere! – and in any language.

Sources

(i) Extract from 'Deor's Lament' (late 9th century); (ii) Extract from John Davidson, 'Thirty Bob a Week' (1894); (iii) Christina Rossetti, 'Twice' (c. 1860); (iv) Stephen Crane, 'In the Desert' (1895); (v) Walt Whitman, extract from 'The Wound-Dresser' (1865); (vi) Emily Dickinson, 'Much Madness Is Divinest Sense' (c. 1862); (vii) Emily Dickinson, 'I Sing to Use the Waiting' (c. 1864); (viii) John Clare, 'I Am' (1846); (ix) John Keats, 'To Autumn' (1819/20); (x) W.H. Auden, 'Stop All the Clocks' (c. 1936); (xi) A.E. Housman, 'Because I Liked You Better' (*publ.* 1936); (xii) John McRae, 'Elijah and Isaac' (1984); (xiii) Langston Hughes, 'I, Too' (1925); (xiv) Maya Angelou, 'Woman Work' (1970s); (xv) Stevie Smith, 'Not Waving But Drowning' (1957); (xvi) Seamus Heaney, 'Digging' (1966); (xvii) Stephen Spender, extract from 'I Think Continually of Those Who Were Truly Great' (1933); (xviii) William Wordsworth, extract from 'Lines Written a Few Miles Above Tintern Abbey' (1798); (xix) Robert Browning, extract from 'Andrea del Sarto' (1855); (xx) Dylan Thomas, extract from 'Do Not Go Gentle into That Good Night' (1952); (xxi) Ella Wheeler Wilcox, extract from 'Solitude' (late 19th century); (xxii) Emma Lazarus, extract from 'The New Colossus' (late 19th century); (xxiii) Walt Whitman, extract from 'Song of Myself', 6 (1855); (xxiv) John Dryden, extract from 'Alexander's Feast' (1697); (xxv) Thomas Wyatt, extract from 'They Flee from Me' (c. 1540); (xxvi) US negro spiritual, traditional; (xxvii) John Milton, extract from *Paradise Lost* (1667); (xxviii) T.S. Eliot, 'extract from The Hollow Men' (1925).

poetry project

As you have gone through this book, you have probably found some poems you like more than others. You could collect them, make your own package of poems, or work on a poetry project around some of them. As you have seen, there are lots of ways of putting texts together - by theme, by author, by time - or just because you like them and they go together. You might also like to record some of them on cassette.

In this final section, the texts are up for grabs. You could group them in any way you like, leave them to stand each on its own, select one or two and leave the rest aside. The package is intended to give you the basis to make up your own selection of poems, in any way you like: maybe to 'sell it' to other people, as an introduction to poetry, or as an overview of some kind (poems on love, on war, or by women, or whatever). Take texts from anywhere - in this book, in others, poems you've written yourself, songs, hymns - and make your own package.

You will notice, for instance, that there is only one poem by a woman here - you might not find that a problem, but you might well want to create a better balance.

This Poetry Project gives you a package of some of the best-known poetry texts in English, with one or two less familiar extras for good measure. First and foremost, they are to be enjoyed, but unfortunately they sometimes also have to be prepared for exams.

As you read them, think constructively about what you could say about each one if you had to discuss it, write about it, or answer an exam question on it. Refer back to anything in the book that might be useful in terms of cross-references, technical words or information. You might want to group some of them into a mini-package - maybe with texts from earlier in the book.

As you look at these ten texts, look for links with others you have read, so that you can make your own package, a Poetry Project linking texts for lots of different reasons - adding new texts, finding texts, or even writing them yourself. This package is to be opened, re-made, cherished, thrown away - whatever! As long as you find one or two (at least!) that you enjoy.

Often considered one of the great texts of its time, and one of the first 'modern' poems, Matthew Arnold's 'Dover Beach' (1867) (Text: Poem (i)) moves from a domestic setting to quite different times and places. As you read, what sights do you see, and what sounds do you hear?

Text: Poem (i)

(i)   The sea is calm tonight.
The tide is full, the moon lies fair
Upon the straits; – on the French coast the light
Gleams and is gone; the cliffs of England stand,
5 Glimmering and vast, out in the tranquil bay.
Come to the window, sweet is the night-air!

Only, from the long line of spray
Where the sea meets the moon-blanch'd land,
Listen! you hear the grating roar
10 Of pebbles which the waves draw back, and fling
At their return, up the high strand,
Begin, and cease, and then again begin,
With tremulous cadence slow, and bring
The eternal note of sadness in.

15 Sophocles long ago
Heard it on the Aegean, and it brought
Into his mind the turbid ebb and flow
Of human misery; we
Find also in the sound a thought,
20 Hearing it by this distant northern sea.

The Sea of Faith
Was once, too, at the full, and round earth's shore
Lay like the folds of a bright girdle furl'd.
But now I only hear
25 Its melancholy, long, withdrawing roar,
Retreating, to the breath
Of the night-wind, down to the vast edges drear
And naked shingles of the world.

> Ah, love, let us be true
> 30   To one another! for the world, which seems
>   To lie before us like a land of dreams,
>   So various, so beautiful, so new,
>   Hath really neither joy, nor love, nor light,
>   Nor certitude, nor peace, nor help for pain;
> 35   And we are here as on a darkling plain
>   Swept with confused alarms of struggle and flight,
>   Where ignorant armies clash by night.

◎   Who is speaking to whom in the opening lines? Where are they?

◎   What is the first connecting word that introduces a contrast to the initial positive atmosphere?

◎   Contrast the first six lines and the last five lines. What movement has there been?

◎   How do the sounds of the sea begin to 'bring /The eternal note of sadness in' (lines 13–14)? What is 'it' (line 16)? How does it link, in time and in distance, with the first section?

◎   Do we need to know who 'Sophocles' (line 15) was?

Extension

◎   As you look at the whole text again, which lines particularly strike you? What is it that you like or find interesting about them?

◎   How much of the poem would you say is emotion, and how much is intellect? Are there other binaries you would want to bring out?

◎   'The Sea of Faith' (line 21) is a phrase that has led to a lot of discussion. The image of the world once being wrapped up tightly in faith, but now 'naked' (line 28), brings together the sea and the 'girdle' (line 23). Do you think we have less 'faith' than earlier ages? What kind of faith do you think the poem implies?

◎   Does the final image suggest a kind of 'waste land' to you? That is a twentieth-century image – but look back to 'When I Have Fears' and 'Ozymandias' (in Unit 3) for earlier hints at it.

'Dover Beach' was published in 1867, eight years after Charles Darwin's *On the Origin of Species*. So it is often related to the mid-Victorian 'crisis of belief', when they could no longer fully believe in the old, received ideas of Creation and the Universe.

◉ Does that information help your reading of the text, or limit it? For you, does the whole poem go beyond that question of faith, or is that its point?

◉ In the final section (lines 29–37), what positives can you find?

◉ 'Ah, love' (line 29) – would it be different if it were just 'Love!'?

◉ Why 'seems' (line 30)? What does 'seems' contrast with?

◉ Do you find the final list of negatives (lines 33–4) realistic, exaggerated, or what?

◉ What overall effect does the poem have on you? Would you accept the judgement that it is a great poem?

Activity

As you read Text: Poem (ii) for the first time, take it realistically. What actually happens?

Text: Poem (ii)

(ii)   Whose woods these are I think I know.
His house is in the village, though;
He will not see me stopping here
To watch his woods fill up with snow.

5 My little horse must think it queer
To stop without a farmhouse near
Between the woods and frozen lake
The darkest evening of the year.

He gives his harness bells a shake
10 To ask if there is some mistake.
The only other sound's the sweep
Of easy wind and downy flake.

The woods are lovely, dark, and deep,
But I have promises to keep,
15 And miles to go before I sleep,
And miles to go before I sleep.

- Does it feel realistic to you? Or do you feel there is more to it? Can you say why?
- Would the effect of the first line be different if it was rewritten as 'I think I know whose woods these are'? Are there other words which give a sense of certainty/uncertainty?
- Who is 'He' (line 3); and 'He' (line 9)?
- How can we tell that 'I' sees the woods positively? Is he attracted to them?
- What sounds and colours do you find?

Extension

This poem has often been interpreted as containing symbols of death. In that reading, the snow is (as it often is) a death symbol, and 'the woods' the unknown territory beyond. Do you find that idea convincing? Or, if it is not that kind of metaphor, is it enough just to see it as a pause on a journey?

What does the repetition of the final lines give you? Decide whether the tone, for you, is hard or soft, determined or resigned, realistic or idealistic.

The centre of the poem is 'The darkest evening of the year' (line 8). How does that contrast with the next line? How long might the pause be between them? This could be seen as tying in with the idea of death.

Activity

Read Text: Poem (iii), and decide how well it goes, or doesn't go, with the poem you have just read.

Text: Poem (iii)

(iii)   Because I could not stop for Death –
        He kindly stopped for me –
        The Carriage held but just Ourselves –
        And Immortality.

     5 We slowly drove – He knew no haste
        And I had put away

129

My labor and my leisure too,
For His Civility -

We passed the School, where Children strove
10   At Recess - in the Ring -
We passed the Fields of Gazing Grain -
We passed the Setting Sun -

Or rather - He passed Us -
The Dews drew quivering and chill -
15   For only Gossamer, my Gown -
My Tippet - only Tulle -

We paused before a House that seemed
A Swelling of the Ground -
The Roof was scarcely visible -
20   The Cornice - in the Ground -

Since then - 'tis Centuries - and yet
Feels shorter than the Day
I first surmised the Horses' Heads
Were toward Eternity -

◎   Is death seen positively or negatively? What words create this image?
◎   Can you trace the movement of time through a day – and through a lifetime?
◎   Who is 'He' (line 13)? What do the next three lines tell you about 'I'? What idea does 'The Carriage' (line 3) and 'the Horses' (line 23) give you?
◎   How do you interpret lines 16–18?
◎   Do you find the rhythm and the rhymes happy or sad? Do they reinforce or seem to contradict the overall theme of the poem?

Extension

The poet Emily Dickinson is famous for her use of multi-syllable words to make a line (see 'Immortality' – line 4 – and 'Civility' – line 8 – above). Does this make the poem seem simpler? Look at the other Dickinson texts you have read (pp. 72–73, 108) and check out the effect there.

This poem has been read as a microcosm of village life – the school, the fields, the graveyard. But, like the Frost text (ii), it could easily be more than that – life, death, and the universe again!

How does the last stanza expand the rest of the poem? Work on binaries, and see what they bring out. Is it more about death or life for you?

Activity

As you read Text: Poem (iv), decide what time of day it is.

Text: Poem (iv)

(iv)   now when the small hours
        grow big with day
        when darkness keeps its perspective
        and the mist of the evening rain waits
5   over bushes and streams
        a small star-petalled flower falls,
        propelling its single flight
        through the dawn-thick air
        folding softly on damp earth,
10   its whiteness caught
        in the late window light.
        death is trivial.

◎   Would it be different without the last line?
◎   Read it again, and trace the movement of the verbs. The only main verb in the first eleven lines is 'falls' (line 6), right at the heart of the text; the others are all subordinate, after 'when' (line 3), or in the continuous form. What does that do to help the idea of the flower?
◎   What kinds of light and dark do you see here? Are there other binaries?
◎   Line 6 is also the poem's title – a good one?
◎   How many of the five senses are involved here? What is this text about, for you?

Commentary

These first four texts could be linked by themes such as death, doubt, symbolism, etc. The 'Dover Beach' idea of standing on the timeless shores, thinking of eternity, could be linked back to Keats (p. 26) and Shelley (p. 35). The idea that love will be the thing to save us could also be pointed up; or the question of what faith is (see the George Herbert poem on pp. 47–48).

The others lend themselves to symbolic readings even more. We have to decide for ourselves how convinced we are that they are symbolic. If the Frost and Dickinson poems make symbols of death, the 'star-petalled flower' in text (iv) combines birth ('grow big with day', line 2) and death. The last line can be read as embodying an Eastern kind of philosophy, where death is just a shift to another state of being – in that case, the poem is an affirmation of life. (The poet is Malaysian and Moslem, which might confirm something of that perspective.)

The next two texts, written at about the same period, show radically different kinds of memory.

Activity

Edward Thomas's 'Adlestrop' (Text: Poem (v)) is about a moment remembered. As you read, see if you can detect a moment when the poem 'takes off'.

Text: Poem (v)

(v)   Yes. I remember Adlestrop –
        The name, because one afternoon
        Of heat the express-train drew up there
        Unwontedly. It was late June.

5   The steam hissed. Someone cleared his throat.
        No one left and no one came
        On the bare platform. What I saw
        Was Adlestrop – only the name

        And willows, willow-herb, and grass,

```
10   And meadowsweet, and haycocks dry,
     No whit less still and lonely fair
     Than the high cloudlets in the sky.

     And for that minute a blackbird sang
     Close by, and round him, mistier,
15   Farther and farther, all the birds
     Of Oxfordshire and Gloucestershire.
```

◎   Why 'Yes' (line 1), do you think? Is it in answer to a question?

◎   The first half of the poem contains quite a few short sentences. What about the second half? Is the vocabulary different?

◎   How does it move from the station? Do you find contrasts between what is named and described in the second half, compared with the first half? And the senses in this one?

◎   Is it helpful to look at binaries, like: particular or specific/general; mechanical/natural; 'late June'/'that minute'; 'hissed'/'sang'; 'bare'/'mistier'; the first line/the last line; past/present; negative/positive; 'Close by'/'farther and farther'? Look at each one and judge how significant you think it is.

◎   There are some fairly unusual words and phrases, like 'Unwontedly' (line 4), 'No whit less still' (line 11), 'lonely fair' (line 11) – combining negative and positive. Is the overall effect *completely* positive, do you think?

◎   Is the poem for you about memory, nostalgia (or both), or what?

Activity

When we looked at 'The Charge of the Light Brigade' (in Unit 7, pp. 94–95) it was clear that it could be interpreted either as a heroic celebration of a battle or as anti-war. Compare that with 'Anthem for Doomed Youth' (in Unit 2, p. 22) – is the prevailing tone anger or sadness or what, in your opinion?

Wilfred Owen described his work in these words: 'The poetry is in the pity.' As you read 'Dulce et Decorum Est' (Text: Poem (vi)), what tone or tones do you detect? The title, by the way, is Latin and means 'It is sweet and noble [to die for one's country]' – the final words of the text.

When does the poem move to remembrance?

Text: Poem (vi)

(vi)   Bent double, like old beggars under sacks,
       Knock-kneed, coughing like hags, we cursed through sludge,
       Till on the haunting flares we turned our backs,
       And towards our distant rest began to trudge.
5   Men marched asleep. Many had lost their boots
       But limped on, blood-shod. All went lame; all blind;
       Drunk with fatigue; deaf even to the hoots
       Of gas-shells dropping softly behind.

       Gas! Gas! Quick, boys! – An ecstasy of fumbling,
10   Fitting the clumsy helmets just in time;
       But someone still was yelling out and stumbling
       And floundering like a man in fire or lime. –
       Dim through the misty panes and thick green light,
       As under a green sea, I saw him drowning.

15   In all my dreams, before my helpless sight,
       He plunges at me, guttering, choking, drowning.

       If in some smothering dreams you too could pace
       Behind the wagon that we flung him in,
       And watch the white eyes writhing in his face,
20   His hanging face, like a devil's sick of sin;
       If you could hear, at every jolt, the blood
       Come gargling from the froth-corrupted lungs,
       Bitter as the cud
       Of vile, incurable sores on innocent tongues, –
25   My friend, you would not tell with such high zest
       To children ardent for some desperate glory,
       The old Lie: Dulce et decorum est
       Pro patria mori.

Commentary

1   There are four stages to the poem, like paragraphs. Before we look
at these, did the rhymes strike you particularly?
      The answer is probably not much – because many of the lines
are **run-on**, that is the sense continues into the next line rather than

finishing at the end of the line; we might notice the rhymes a bit less than we did in 'The Charge of the Light Brigade' and 'Anthem for Doomed Youth'.

Trace the rhymes back from the final line before you read the poem again.

2   Now look at the final section. Who is 'you' (lines 17, 21)? And who is 'him' (line 18)? When is 'you' addressed directly again? The relationship between the reader, the dead man and the poet is vital to the impact of the poem.

3   When is 'him' first mentioned? What has happened to him? What did he fail to do (lines 10–11)?

Who are 'we' (lines 2, 3)? Do they look and march like soldiers? What words in particular convey their condition to you? You could probably find *opposites* to traditional military images. You might look at nouns ('beggars', 'hags'), adjectives ('blind', 'drunk'), or verbs ('cursed', 'trudge'). What does 'blood-shod' (line 6) mean?

4   As in 'Anthem for Doomed Youth', the sounds and colours are significant. Check out the sounds and colours in lines 1–12. And, again, check how many of the senses are brought in.

At line 15, the text moves from the past tense to the present. Memory, and the continuation of memory, begins to become important.

5   The final section, from line 17, all depends on 'If'. How important that 'If' is for 'you' in the text becomes the main thrust of the poem, and the reader is made to feel and see what the poet describes.

Line 23 is a half-line – only five syllables, while all the other lines have ten. Does it make you stop for a moment as you read? Remember 'these who die as cattle' in 'Anthem for Doomed Youth' – again Owen uses '*as*' rather than 'like', stressing that it *is*, not is like.

The only other short line is the last one. Why is it a 'Lie' (line 27), with a capital L? Who tells it, when? It brings us back to questions we saw earlier about 'glory' in this 'Lie', and in Tennyson's 'The Charge of the Light Brigade'.

6   There are lots of surprising, original words and combinations of words you might pick out in this text: 'an ecstasy of fumbling' (line 9) is a striking contrast; 'froth-corrupted lungs' (line 22) a description that carries on the gargling sound. Are there others you would point to as particularly effective, or strange, or puzzling?

Extension

The rhythm and tone of this text are quite different from those of 'The Charge of the Light Brigade' and 'Anthem for Doomed Youth'. If you were to choose adjectives to describe them from this list, how would you relate your choice to the *language* of each text? (Probably each adjective would only apply to one of the texts. You can add others.)

elegiac   documentary   rhythmic   sonorous   enthusiastic
sad   critical   disgusted   mourning   reflective   bitter
unheroic   heroic

How does each of the three poems point towards the future?

Activity

Text: Poem (vii) is full of images of chaos and endings. Is there any sign of hope in it?

Text: Poem (vii)

(vii)   Turning and turning in the widening gyre
         The falcon cannot hear the falconer;
         Things fall apart; the centre cannot hold;
         Mere anarchy is loosed upon the world,
    5   The blood-dimmed tide is loosed, and everywhere
         The ceremony of innocence is drowned;
         The best lack all conviction, while the worst
         Are full of passionate intensity.

         Surely some revelation is at hand;
    10   Surely the Second Coming is at hand.
         The Second Coming! Hardly are those words out
         When a vast image out of *Spiritus Mundi*
         Troubles my sight: somewhere in sands of the desert
         A shape with lion body and the head of a man,
    15   A gaze blank and pitiless as the sun,
         Is moving its slow thighs, while all about it
         Reel shadows of the indignant desert birds.

> The darkness drops again; but now I know
> That twenty centuries of stony sleep
> 20 Were vexed to nightmare by a rocking cradle,
> And what rough beast, its hour come round at last,
> Slouches towards Bethlehem to be born?

Commentary

1   The first image can be read quite simply: as the falcon soars higher and higher in its spiral, it goes out of human control. Does that tie in with the images in lines 3–8?

What lines struck you particularly? What kinds of violence do you find in lines 3–6? Who could 'The best' and 'the worst' (line 7) be, in your opinion?

2   The title of the poem is introduced in line 10 (and 11). What does it suggest to you? Should it be positive or negative?

What happens to the poet's idea of the Second Coming?

What do you think *Spiritus Mundi* (line 12) might be? (The words mean the Spirit of the World.) Is the image vivid to you? (Yeats himself described *Spiritus Mundi* as 'A general storehouse of images which have ceased to be the property of any personality or spirit'. Does that help?)

3   The movement at the beginning ('turning', 'widening', line 1) turns into different shapes towards the end. 'Reel' (line 17), 'rocking' (line 20), and 'Slouches' (line 22) all move towards an 'out-of-control' kind of movement.

4   The end of the twentieth century has been seen as the end of a cycle, or gyre – and this has led to a flurry of interpretations of this poem. How negative do you find it? Check back to Shelley's 'Ozymandias' in Unit 3 – you might find similarities or echoes.

Line 20 might be seen as echoing Whitman's line 'Out of the cradle endlessly rocking'. Do you find this and the Shelley echoes valid?

The Nigerian writer Chinua Achebe used *Things Fall Apart* (see line 3) as the title of his novel about the fragmentation of African tribal values: is this appropriate, in your opinion, or just theft?

What is this poem most about for you – violence, religion, the future, nightmares, the end of the world, or what?

137

Activity

Text: Poem (viii) is about family. As you read, see if you think the poet's right or not.

Text: Poem (viii)

> (viii)   They fuck you up, your mum and dad.
> They may not mean to, but they do.
> They fill you with the faults they had
> And add some extra, just for you.
>
> 5   But they were fucked up in their turn
> By fools in old-style hats and coats,
> Who half the time were soppy-stern
> And half at one another's throats.
>
> Man hands on misery to man.
> 10 It deepens like a coastal shelf.
> Get out as early as you can,
> And don't have any kids yourself.

- Well, do they? And were they?
- What is the image you get from 'soppy-stern' (line 7)? What does this old-fashioned image look like?
- How is the third stanza different?
- How do you react to line 10? Is the image a good one?
- Do you find the final lines funny, realistic, cynical, bleak, or what?
- So, what does the first line imply, in your own words? Why do you think the poet used an expression like this? Is it 'unpoetic'?

The title Philip Larkin gave this is 'This Be the Verse', which has caused some perplexity. It is taken from the 'Requiem' section of *Underwoods* by Robert Louis Stevenson (Text: Poem (ix)).

Text: Poem (ix)

(ix)   Under the wide and starry sky
Dig the grave and let me lie.
Gladly did I live and gladly die,
      And I laid me down with a will.
This be the verse you grave for me:
'Here he lies where he longed to be;
Home is the sailor, home from sea,
      And the hunter home from the hill.'

Does that fit in with the Larkin poem for you? If not, can you give any ideas for Larkin's choice of title? Is it an epitaph? Is it ironic?

Activity

As you read the final text (poem (x)), what minorities can you find?

Text: Poem (x)

(x)   The most famous violinist on Eigg,
Denounced from the pulpit for his Gaelic folksongs,

Threw on the fire an instrument made
By a pupil of Stradivarius.

5 'The sooner,' thundered *The Times*,
'All Welsh specialities disappear

From the face of the earth the better.'
You whose parents came from a valley

North of Hanoi are now living in Princeton
10 Teaching low-temperature physics. Often

When you spoke about poems in Vietnamese
I heard behind the pride in your voice

Like a ceilidh in an unexpected place
The burning violins of small peoples.

◎ How much do you need to know the references – to 'Eigg' (line 1), 'Stradivarius' (line 4), 'low-temperature physics' (line 10) – to understand the text?

◎ How does line 2 link with line 5?

◎ How do past and present relate?

◎ Does the last line refer to the whole poem?

Eigg is an island in the Inner Hebrides; Stradivarius made violins in Cremona in the seventeenth century; *The Times* (line 5) used to be called 'the Thunderer'; 'ceilidh' (line 13) is a Gaelic word for a communal singing and dancing party. What does 'the pulpit' (line 2) have to do with any of these?

The title of this poem is 'Nec Tamen Consumebatur'. It is a reference to the Biblical story in the Book of Exodus about the burning bush: and it was not consumed (by fire). It is also the motto of the Church of Scotland (and, as such, is seen on the pulpit-fall, the cloth covering the pulpit, in many Scottish churches).

A poem about minorities, with a wide range of cultural and geographical references – sums up the whole book in a way.

Extension 1

With any text you discuss, look first at what the form and the language tell you, then seek out a few binaries, check the first line/last line movement – and you've already got quite a lot to say. These will give you a solid, objective basis, and you can go on to rather more subjective areas such as effects, themes, and interpretations. But check out rhymes, rhythm, parallelism, syntactic patterns objectively too, to make sure you don't go off at a tangent.

Whatever you do, *never* try to say what the author meant – say what you think the text means.

This checklist covers many of the things you will want to look at:

form – the look of the text; metre and rhyme; stanzas; run-on lines; sonnet; ballad; punctuation

sound – fast or slow; alliteration; assonance; stress; rhyme and rhythm; the music of the text, etc.

words – familiar or unfamiliar, simple or complex, Anglo-Saxon or Latinate, concrete or abstract

images – connotations, similes and metaphors

voices – obvious or hidden, whose are they, I/you/others?

tone – serious, light, ironic, polemical, lyrical
content – abstract, realistic, descriptive, thematic, time/place
interpretation – open, multi-level, simplistic, subjective/objective
appeal – what kind of impact does it have? emotional, rational, etc.
There can be more!

Extension 2

As a final check-out, why not go back to the idea in Unit 1 of giving points to some of the poems you have read. Is it easy to give them marks on a 1–10 scale? Try to make your own personal Top Ten of the texts you have read.

Sources

(i) Matthew Arnold, 'Dover Beach' (1867); (ii) Robert Frost, 'Stopping by Woods on a Snowy Evening' (1923); (iii) Emily Dickinson, 'Because I Could Not Stop for Death' (c. 1863); (iv) Muhammad Haji Salleh, 'A Star-Petalled Flower Falls' (1978); (v) Edward Thomas, 'Adlestrop' (1915); (vi) Wilfred Owen, 'Dulce et Decorum Est' (1917); (vii) W.B. Yeats, 'The Second Coming' (1919); (viii) Philip Larkin, 'This Be the Verse' (1974); (ix) Robert Louis Stevenson, 'Requiem' from *Underwoods* (1887); (x) Robert Crawford, 'Nec Tamen Consumebatur' (1990)

list of texts

Dates given are for the year or approximate year of composition; occasionally, the date of first publication, when known, is given, preceded by *publ.*

Unit 1

(i)   Anonymous obituary verse

(ii)   William Wordsworth, extract from ' 'Tis Said That Some Have Died for Love' (1800)

(iii)   William Wordsworth, extract from 'The Thorn' (early draft, 1798)

(iv)   Edward Clerihew Bentley, 'Clive' from *Biography for Beginners* (1905)

(v)   Extract from UK national anthem (18th century)

(vi)   Edward Lear, extract from *One Hundred Nonsense Pictures and Rhymes* (1872)

(vii)   William Shakespeare, extract from *Cymbeline* (1610)

(viii)   William McGonagall, extract from 'The Famous Tay Whale' (1883/4)

(ix)   Elizabeth Barrett Browning, extract from *Sonnets from the Portuguese*, 43 (1850)

(x)   Anonymous advertising slogan (1880s)

(xi)   Christopher Marlowe, extract from *Hero and Leander* (*publ.* 1598)

(xii)   Edmund Spenser, extract from *Prothalamion* (1596)

(xiii)   William Shakespeare, extract from *Sonnets*, 18 (*c.* 1594)

(xiv)   William Blake, extract from 'The Tyger' from *Songs of Innocence and Experience* (1794)

(xv)   13th-century English lyric

(xvi)   Walt Whitman, extract from 'When Lilacs Last in the Dooryard Bloomed' (1865)

(xvii)   Alfred, Lord Tennyson, extract from 'Tithonus' (1833)

(xviii)   William Carlos Williams, 'This Is Just to Say' (1923)

(xix)   Roger McGough, '40-Love' (1971)

(xx)   John Milton, extract from *Paradise Lost* (1667)

(xxi)   John McRae, 'The Fire That Burned' (1993)

(xxii)   George Gordon, Lord Byron, extract from 'When We Two Parted' (*c.* 1820)

(xxiii)   Lewis Carroll, extract from *Through the Looking Glass* (1871)

(xxiv)   Thomas Hood, extract from 'Faithless Nelly Gray' (1820s)

Unit 2

(i)   John Keats, extract from 'La Belle Dame sans Merci' (1819/20)

(ii)   William Shakespeare, extract from *Sonnets*, 87 (*c.* 1594)

(iii)   Anonymous, 'The Queen's Marys' (16th century)

(iv)   Wilfred Owen, extract from 'Strange Meeting' (*c.* 1917)

(v)   George W. Young, extract from 'The Lips that Touched Liquor Must Never Touch Mine' (*c.* 1900)

(vi)   Alfred, Lord Tennyson, extract from 'The Brook' (1864)

(vii)   John Keats, extract from 'Ode to a Nightingale' (1819)

(viii)   Andrew Marvell, extract from 'To His Coy Mistress' (1670s)

(ix)   Percy Bysshe Shelley, extract from 'The Cloud' (1820)

(x)   Philip Sidney, extract from *Astrophel and Stella*, 31 (*publ.* 1591)

(xi)   Francis Thompson, extract from 'To a Snowflake' (1890s)

(xii)   Henry Vaughan, extract from 'They Are All Gone' (1655)

(xiii)   William Blake, 'The Fly' from *Songs of Innocence and Experience* (1789/94)

(xiv)   Rupert Brooke, extract from 'The Soldier' (1915)

(xv)   Samuel Taylor Coleridge, extract from 'The Rime of the Ancient Mariner' (1798)

(xvi)   Thomas Gray, extract from 'Elegy Written in a Country Churchyard' (1750/1)

(xvii)   W.S. Gilbert, extract from *The Pirates of Penzance* (1879)

(xviii)   Gavin Ewart, 'Office Friendships' (1966)

(xix)   William Shakespeare, *Sonnets*, 144 (*c.* 1594)

(xx)   Wilfred Owen, 'Anthem for Doomed Youth' (1918)

Unit 3

(i)   John Keats, 'When I Have Fears' (1818)

(ii)   Gerard Manley Hopkins, 'Carrion Comfort' (*c.* 1885)

(iii)   Thomas Wyatt, 'I Find No Peace' (*c.* 1540)

(iv)   Gerard Manley Hopkins, 'No Worst' (*c.* 1885)

(v)   William Wordsworth, 'Daffodils' (1804/15)

(vi)   Percy Bysshe Shelley, 'Ozymandias' (1818)

Unit 4

(i)   Anonymous, 'Lord Randal' (15th century)

(ii)   John Bunyan, extract from 'To Be a Pilgrim' (1678)

(iii)   Robert Burns, extract from 'Auld Lang Syne' (1786)

(iv)   Anonymous, 'Poor Men Pay for All' (1640s)

(v)   Thomas Hood, 'extract from The Song of the Shirt' (1843)

(vi)   George Crabbe, extract from 'The Village' (1783)

(vii)   Edward Fitzgerald, extract from *The Rubaiyat of Omar Khayyam* (1859)

(viii)   Rudyard Kipling, extract from 'If' (1910)

(ix)   John Donne, 'The Good Morrow' (*c.* 1600)

(x)   George Herbert, 'The Collar' (1620s)

Unit 5

(i)   Tom Leonard, 'Just ti Let Yi No' (1975)

(ii)   Valerie Bloom, 'Yuh Hear Bout' (1983)

(iii) e.e. cummings, 'ygUDuh' (*c.* 1930)

(iv) Malachi Edwin Vethamani, 'It Was a Wondrous Sight' (1991)

(v) A.P. Graves, extract from 'Father O'Flynn' (1889)

(vi) Benjamin Zephaniah, 'As a African' (1988)

(vii) Louise Bennett, 'Colonization in Reverse' (1982)

(viii) E.J. Overbury, 'The Springtime It Brings On the Shearing' (late 19th century)

(ix) William Barnes, extract from 'Lwonesomeness' (1861)

(x) Nissim Ezekiel, 'Goodbye Party for Miss Pushpa T.S.' (1976)

(xi) Alfred, Lord Tennyson, extract from 'Northern Farmer, New Style' (1847)

(xii) Robert Burns, 'To a Mouse' (1785)

(xiii) Tony Harrison, 'Them and [uz]' (1978)

Unit 6

(i) Mehetabel Wright, extract from 'Address to Her Husband' (*c.* 1730)

(ii) Sarah Egerton, extract from 'The Repulse to Alcander' (1703)

(iii) Charlotte Smith, 'Fragment Descriptive of the Miseries of War' (1797)

(iv) Anne Bradstreet, extract from 'Verses Upon the Burning of Our House' (1666)

(v) Rebecca Hughes, 'Divergence' (1996)

(vi) Emily Dickinson, 'A Narrow Fellow in the Grass' (*c.* 1865)

(vii) Amy Lowell, 'Patterns' (1916)

(viii) Christina Rossetti, extract from 'A Pause of Thought' (*c.* 1860)

(ix) Lady Mary Wortley Montagu, extract from 'To the Imitator of the First Satire of Horace' (*c.* 1734)

(x) Hilary Tham, 'Offerings' (1976)

(xi) Lady Mary Chudleigh, extract from 'To the Ladies' (1703)

(xii) Lorna Goodison, 'I Am Becoming My Mother' (1986)

(xiii) Robert Browning, 'Porphyria's Lover' (1836)

(xiv) Arthur Hugh Clough, extract from 'How Pleasant It Is to Have Money' from *Dipsychus* (1850/1)

(xv) John Keats, 'La Belle Dame sans Merci' (1819/20)

(xvi) Samuel Taylor Coleridge, extract from 'The Rime of the Ancient Mariner' (1798)

Unit 7

(i) e.e. cummings, extract from 'N&: VII' (1925)

(ii) William Shakespeare, extract from '*As You Like It*' (1599/1600)

(iii) Song title, 1960

(iv) W.E. Henley, extract from 'To W.R.' from *Echoes* (1888)

(v) John Dryden, extract from 'The Medal' (1682)

(vi) John Gay, 'My Own Epitaph' (1720)

(vii) Song title, 1966

(viii) Robert Burns, extract from 'My Love Is Like a Red, Red Rose' (*c.* 1796)

(ix) Francis Quarles, extract from 'Emblems' (1643)

(x) Jonathan Swift, extract from 'On Poetry' (1733)

(**xi**)   Algernon Swinburne, extract from 'Atalanta in Calydon' (1865)

(**xii**)   Richard Lovelace, extract from 'To Althea from Prison' (1642)

(**xiii**)   James Elroy Flecker, extract from 'Hassan' (1922)

(**xiv**)   Ernest Dowson, 'Vitae Summa Brevis Spem Nos Vetat Incohare Longam' (1896)

(**xv**)   Simon Armitage, 'Let This Matchstick Be a Brief Biography' (1995)

(**xvi**)   William Blake, 'Auguries of Innocence' (c. 1803)

(**xvii**)   Alfred, Lord Tennyson, 'The Charge of the Light Brigade' (1854)

(**xviii**)   Oscar Wilde, extract from *The Ballad of Reading Gaol* (1898)

(**xix**)   John Taylor, 'The Trumpet of Liberty' (1791)

(**xx**)   William Wordsworth, extract from 'The French Revolution As It Appeared to Enthusiasts' (1809) and *The Prelude*

(**xxi**)   William Dunbar, extract from 'Lament for the Makers' (c. 1507)

Unit 8

(**i**)   Extract from 'Deor's Lament' (late 9th century)

(**ii**)   Extract from John Davidson, 'Thirty Bob a Week' (1894)

(**iii**)   Christina Rossetti, 'Twice' (c. 1860)

(**iv**)   Stephen Crane, 'In the Desert' (1895)

(**v**)   Walt Whitman, extract from 'The Wound-Dresser' (1865)

(**vi**)   Emily Dickinson, 'Much Madness Is Divinest Sense' (c. 1862)

(**vii**)   Emily Dickinson, 'I Sing to Use the Waiting' (c. 1864)

(**viii**)   John Clare, 'I Am' (1846)

(**ix**)   John Keats, 'To Autumn' (1819/20)

(**x**)   W.H. Auden, 'Stop All the Clocks' (c. 1936)

(**xi**)   A.E. Housman, 'Because I Liked You Better' (*publ.* 1936)

(**xii**)   John McRae, 'Elijah and Isaac' (1984)

(**xiii**)   Langston Hughes, 'I, Too' (1925)

(**xiv**)   Maya Angelou, 'Woman Work' (1970s)

(**xv**)   Stevie Smith, 'Not Waving But Drowning' (1957)

(**xvi**)   Seamus Heaney, 'Digging' (1966)

(**xvii**)   Stephen Spender, extract from 'I Think Continually of Those Who Were Truly Great' (1933)

(**xviii**)   Extract from William Wordsworth, 'Lines Written a Few Miles Above Tintern Abbey' (1798)

(**xix**)   Robert Browning, extract from 'Andrea del Sarto' (1855)

(**xx**)   Dylan Thomas, extract from 'Do Not Go Gentle into That Good Night' (1952)

(**xxi**)   Ella Wheeler Wilcox, extract from 'Solitude' (late 19th century)

(**xxii**)   Emma Lazarus, extract from 'The New Colossus' (late 19th century)

(**xxiii**)   Walt Whitman, extract from 'Song of Myself', 6 (1855)

(**xxiv**)   John Dryden, extract from 'Alexander's Feast' (1697)

(**xxv**)   Thomas Wyatt, extract from 'They Flee from Me' (c. 1540) (**xxvi**) US negro spiritual, traditional

(**xxvii**) John Milton, extract from *Paradise Lost* (1667)

(**xxviii**) T.S. Eliot, 'extract from The Hollow Men' (1925)

Poetry project

(**i**) Matthew Arnold, 'Dover Beach' (1867)

(**ii**) Robert Frost, 'Stopping by Woods on a Snowy Evening' (1923)

(**iii**) Emily Dickinson, 'Because I Could Not Stop for Death' (*c*. 1863)

(**iv**) Muhammad Haji Salleh, 'A Star-Petalled Flower Falls' (1978)

(**v**) Edward Thomas, 'Adlestrop' (1915)

(**vi**) Wilfred Owen, 'Dulce et Decorum Est' (1917)

(**vii**) W.B. Yeats, 'The Second Coming' (1919)

(**viii**) Philip Larkin, 'This Be the Verse' (1974)

(**ix**) Robert Louis Stevenson, 'Requiem' from *Underwoods* (1887)

(**x**) Robert Crawford, 'Nec Tamen Consumebatur' (1990)

index of terms

This is a form of combined glossary and index. Listed below are some of the main key terms used in the book, together with brief definitions for purposes of reference. The page references will normally take you to the first use of the term in the book where it will be shown in **bold**. In some cases, however, understanding of the term can be helped by exploring its uses in more than one place in the book and accordingly more than one page reference is given.

149

which rhyme, and usually have the same rhythm.

culture (high and low) 39

These concepts have come to relate to art at an intellectual level (high culture), which has a different origin and appeal from low culture, which tends to refer to popular art, music and writing.

dialect 53

A language variety in which the use of grammar and vocabulary identify the regional or social background of the speaker. People in the West Midlands of England will say 'her's saft' rather than 'she's daft'; 'saft' combined from 'soft' and 'daft'; 'her' used instead of 'she' (see **accent**).

epic 9

A long text, usually on a grand scale, concerning weighty moral or historical themes.

eye-rhyme (see **rhyme**)

free verse 11

Poetry which has no regular rhyme, rhythm or line length, but depends on the flow of natural spoken language.

function word 19

A word whose role is largely or wholly to express a grammatical relationship, such as 'to' or 'and' (see also **content word**).

haiku 9

A Japanese verse form of seventeen syllables; successful examples capture the essence, or 'zen', of a single moment or incident.

iambic pentameter 9

A regular poetic rhythm in which the lines contain five stressed syllables, preceded by five unstressed syllables. An *iamb* is a *metrical foot* (see **scansion**) written down as ∪ –, and this is repeated five times ('penta' = five, in Greek) in iambic pentameter. Other metrical feet include the *anapaest* (short-short-long, ∪ ∪ –), the *dactyl* (long-short-short, – ∪ ∪), the *spondee* (long-long, – –), and the *trochee* (long-short, – ∪). Other line lengths include *hexameter* (six feet) and *heptameter* (seven feet).

internal rhyme (see **rhyme**)

metaphor 90

A word or phrase which establishes a comparison or analogy between one object or idea and another. 'All the world's a stage', for example contains a comparison between the world and a stage, underlining the idea that everything we do is a performance of some kind (see **simile**).

metaphysical 50

A term first used by the eighteenth-century critic Doctor Samuel Johnson, to describe the complex issues and language of such early seventeenth-century poets as John Donne and George Herbert (see Unit 4, texts *(ix)* and *(x)*). Metaphysics is actually the philosophical science of the first principles of nature and thought. Johnson used the term pejoratively, finding these poets needlessly obscure; but the early twentieth-century poet and critic, T.S. Eliot, largely rehabilitated the reputation of the metaphysical poets.

octet (see **sonnet**)

paradox 15

A striking juxtaposition of apparently contradictory or incompatible words; for example, W.B. Yeats (in 'Easter 1916') mentions 'A terrible beauty'.

parallelism 25

The use of partial repetition to express similar but often contrasting ideas.

personification 114

Giving values and feelings typical to human beings to other animals, or even inanimate objects or concepts.

pun 11

Also called *word play*. This is the use of a word or phrase which has more than one meaning, and a double or multiple meaning is implied. 'Arms', for example, in Thomas Hood's 'Faithless Nelly Gray' (Unit 1, text (xxiv)), can be read as both 'weapons' (literally) and 'limbs' (jokingly). The effect is usually intended to be humorous.

received pronunciation 65

The regionally neutral prestige pronunciation of modern British English.

representational language 92

Any use of words which requires an intellectual and/or emotional response, and interpretation beyond their literal meaning. Images, **metaphors**, and **similes** are all examples of representational language.

refrain 94

The repetition of a line or lines through a poetic text; sometimes also called a *chorus*. In songs, the verse would be

sung by a soloist, the refrain or chorus by the assembled company.

rhyme 3

The matching of words or syllables which, when spoken, have the same sound; e.g. how/now/cow. Rhymes in poetry usually come at the end of lines (see **rhyme scheme**). **Internal rhyme** occurs where two or more words within a line of poetry rhyme; for example, 'Tell' and 'well' in Shelley's 'Ozymandias' (p. 35). **Eye-rhyme** is where words are spelled similarly, but the pronunciation does not make a rhyme; an example might be bough/cough/enough.

rhyme scheme 9

The succession of rhymes at the end of lines in a poetic text. These are written down using letters of the alphabet: for example, the rhyme scheme of a Shakespeare sonnet is

a b a b c d c d e f e f g g.

rhythm 9

The pattern of stressed and unstressed (or weak) syllables in a text. (See also **iambic pentameter** and **scansion**.)

run-on 136

Where the sense, language and rhythm of lines of poetry continue uninterrupted from one line to the next.

scansion 114

The marking of a poetic text into stressed and unstressed syllables, respectively notated as – and ∪ Also, the division of lines into metrical feet (see **iambic pentameter**); for example, the scansion of a line of iambic pentameter would be:

∪ - / ∪ - / ∪ - / ∪ - / ∪ -

sestet   (see **sonnet**)

simile   92
> A simile makes a comparison with the use of such words as 'like' or 'as', for example 'Love is like a violin' (see **metaphor**).

sonnet   23
> A poem of fourteen lines, with regular rhythm and rhyme, and usually with a single theme. Sonnets are often divided into an **octet**, the first eight lines which present the theme, and a **sestet**, lines 9–14, which come to a resolution or conclusion. Shakespearian sonnets typically finish with a **couplet**.

sprung rhythm   29
> The mixing of metrical feet (see **iambic pentameter**) in lines of poetry, especially the proliferation of unstressed syllables. Common in medieval verse, it was characteristic of the poetry of Hopkins (Unit 3, texts (ii) and (iv)).

standard/non-standard English   63
> Varieties of English which are considered to be the norm (standard), or not conforming to the norm (non-standard).

stanza   11
> The grouping of lines of poetry within a complete poetic text – also sometimes called a 'verse'. For example, Wordsworth's 'Daffodils' (p. 33) comprises four stanzas of six lines each.

syllable   9
> A single sound, combined in words (for instance, po-e-try is 3 syllables) and lines or sentences: 'The trum-pets sound-ed' (Unit 1, text (i)) has a syllable count of five.

syntax   8
> The way in which words are put together grammatically.

index of authors